HISTORY OF THE CHAITANYA FAITH IN ORISSA

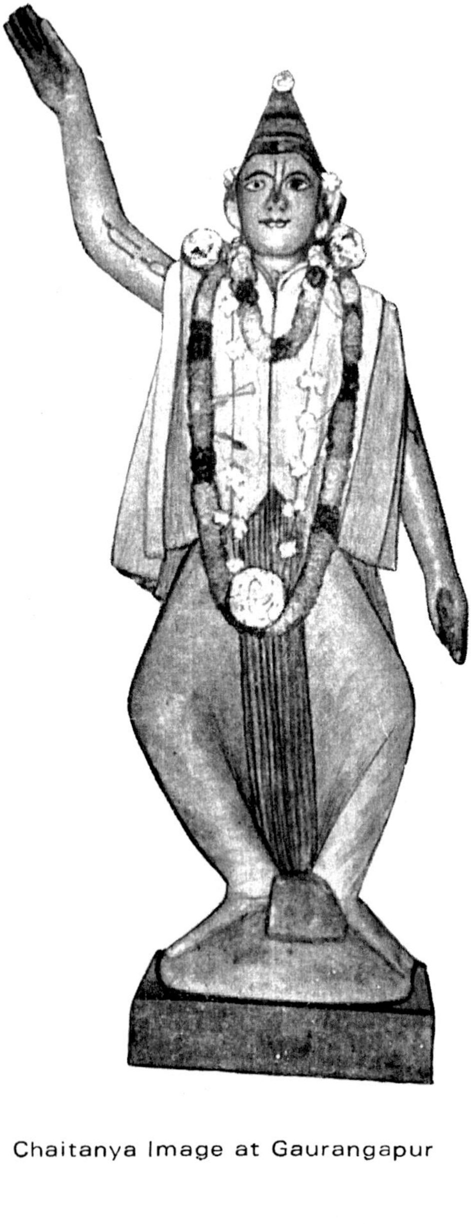

Chaitanya Image at Gaurangapur

History of the Chaitanya Faith in Orissa

PRABHAT MUKHERJEE

MANOHAR
2026

First published 1979
Reprinted 2023, 2024, 2025, 2026

ISBN 978-93-94262-38-6

Published by
Ajay Kumar Jain for
Manohar Publishers & Distributors
4753/23 Ansari Road, Daryaganj
New Delhi 110 002

Printed at
Replika Press Pvt. Ltd.

TO THE MEMORY OF

DR ANNCHARLOTT ESCHMANN

WHO MADE OUTSTANDING CONTRIBUTION

TO THE STUDY OF THE RELIGIOUS HERITAGE OF ORISSA

BEFORE HER PREMATURE DEATH

Preface

Chaitanya is probably the only Hindu saint, who was deified during his life time. The belief in his divinity was caused by his extraordinarily fair complexion and outstanding religious personality. Chaitanya, after taking sannyāsa, stayed for the rest of his life mostly at Puri in Orissa. The term, 'Bengal' or 'Gauḍīya' is commonly, but to some extent incorrectly, applied to the religious movement which he started. Sufficient materials are not available for the history of the last years of Chaitanya. We have to depend largely on the embellished biography of Chaitanya, which Kṛishṇadās Kaviraj wrote for the Vaishṇavas in Bengal.

History of monasticism during this period requires further study. It appears that Īśvar, a Vaishṇava, took initiation from Mādhavendra Puri by reciting the *mahavākya* of the Śankarite Puri order, in order to become a monk. Similarly, Mādhavendra, a Vaishṇava, was ordained a monk of the Śankarite Puri order. Was there no provision for monkhood in Vaishṇavism?

I have made use of the late Dr. B.B. Majumdar's book in Bengali entitled *Chaitanya Chariter Upādān* for which I express my indebtedness to him. It is my melancholy duty to recall the memory of late Dr. Anncharlott Eschmann. She made many useful suggestions. I express my deep gratitude to Dr. Hermann Kulke of the South Asia Institute of the Heidelberg University, who is at present the Visiting Professor of History at the Utkal University, Bhubaneswar for taking keen interest in my work. Shri Nityananda Mahapatra, Dr. B. Venkataraman I.A.S. and Shri Biswanath Das also assisted me.

I am grateful to the German Research Council at Bonn for financing the work and to the South Asia Institute at Heidelberg for subsidising the publication. I should also thank Shri Ramesh Jain, the publisher, for his unfailing courtesy.

PRABHAT MUKHERJEE
15 Satyanagar
Bhubaneswar
(Orissa)

13 March 1979
Dolayatra

Contents

PREFACE		vii
I.	Important literary sources on Chaitanya in Sanskrit and Bengali	1
II.	Chaitanya in Oriya literature	11
III.	Chaitanya in Orissa	19
IV.	The Passing Away of Chaitanya	42
V.	Chaitanya and Jagannāth	48
	Appendix—Chaitanya as the Embodiment of Buddha-Jagannāth	54
VI.	Religious Outlook of Chaitanya	56
VII.	Chaitanya's association with Five Comrades	62
	Appendix—Differences between the Chaitanya faith and Orissan Vaishṇavism	69
VIII.	Other Oriya Followers of Chaitanya	73
IX.	Chaitanya's Influence on History of Orissa	
	Section 1—Political condition	80
	Section 2—Society	83
	Section 3—Religion	84
X.	History of Vaishṇavism in Orissa in the 16th century	
	Section 1—Jagannāth	88
	Section 2—Prominent Gauḍiya followers	90
	Section 3—Some followers of Chaitanya	95
XI.	The Post-Chaitanya Oriya Vaishṇava literature	98
XII.	The Spread of the Chaitanya Movement in Orissa	102
XIII.	Chaitanya Worship Today	
	Section 1—Objects	111
	Section 2—Places associated with his memory	112
	Section 3—The Chaitanya temples	113
BIBLIOGRAPHY		117
GLOSSARY		120
GLOSSARY OF MYTHOLOGICAL PERSONS		121
INDEX		122
INDEX OF LITERARY SOURCES		125

CHAPTER I

Literary Sources on Chaitanya in Sanskrit and Bengali

THE SANSKRIT BIOGRAPHIES OF CHAITANYA

CHAITANYA is one of the few Saints in India regarding whom detailed information is available from the literary sources. The five important biographies of Chaitanya were written within eighty years of his death in A.D. 1533. These works contain historical information; varied nature of which reflects the inclinations of their authors. These writers deified Chaitanya and started miraculous legends in his name to prove his divinity.[1]

Nevertheless, the works of Murāri Gupta and Paramānanda Sen popularly known as Kavikarṇapūra, in Sanskrit and of Vṛindāvan Dās and Kṛishṇadās Kavirāj in Bengali throw considerable light on Chaitanya and his age. From these sources we get a reliable picture of an extra-ordinary religious personality, whose teachings have left permanent impressions upon the religious history of Bengal and Orissa. Murāri Gupta and Kavikarṇapūra knew Chaitanya. Vṛindāvan Dās and probably Jayananda consulted persons who were closely associated with the Master. The Sanskrit biographies of Chaitanya depict him as an

---

[1]Murāri Gupta, an associate of Chaitanya, describes the Saint in his work the *Chaitanya Charitāmṛita* as 'four-handed Vishṇu' (I.1.14). Murāri writes that the gods sang in praise of Chaitanya when he was in his mother's womb (I.5. 6-16). Nine years after the passing away of Chaitanya, Kavikarṇapūra writes in his poetical work (kāvya), under the same title the *Chaitanya Charitāmṛita* that Chaitanya is 'the Lord of the Gopīs' (milk-maids of Vṛindāvana) I.8. The drama of Kavikarṇapūra refers to the manifestation of Kṛishṇa in the form of Chaitanya (IV.46). "All his (Vṛindāvan Dās's) inspirations came from the *Bhāgavata* and in every action of the Master, he finds a repetition of Kṛishṇa's doings' (Dr. D.C. Sen: *Chaitanya and His Age*, p. 75). Kṛishṇa-dās Kavirāj in his *Chaitanya Charitāmṛita* (to be abbreviated as *Ch. Ch.*) even makes tigers and deer recite the name of Kṛishṇa in the presence of Chaitanya (II.17.37).

Chaitanya, who was called the Master (*Mahāprabhu*) by his devotees manifested himself as Kṛishṇa with four hands (*Ch. Ch.* II.6.183 and II.10.31). He appeared as the dual incarnation of Rādhā and Kṛishṇa before Rāmānanda (*Ch. Ch.* II.8.230).

ordinary man also.[2] But the important Bengali biographies of Chaitanya were written from devotional point of view, in the interests of the Chaitanya faith, the dogmas of which were described with precision. Events and happenings were, therefore, exaggerated for the glorification of Chaitanya and his sect.

Murāri Gupta's *Chaitanya Charitāmṛita* is the earliest known biographical work on Chaitanya. Murāri studied in the same Sanskrit school with Viśvambhar (Chaitanya's name before he became a monk). Chaitanya went into trance for the first time in Murāri's house at Navadvīpa.

Murāri Gupta's book ends with Chaitanya's return from Vṛindāvana. Subsequently, it was elaborated by the addition of fresh notes by someone else.[3]

Paramānanda Sen, better known by his literary title Kavikarṇapūra ("the ear ornaments of the poets") was the son of Śivānanda Sen, an intimate follower of Chaitanya. Kavikarṇapūra in his childhood saw Chaitanya. Śivānanda Sen first came to Orissa in 1513, and then frequently during the chariot festivals. Thus Kavikarṇapūra obtained information about Chaitanya from his father. While in his teens, he composed the *Chaitanya Charitāmṛita kāvya* in 1542. In this kāvya, he closely followed the account of Murāri Gupta. His second work, the *Chaitanya Chandrodaya* drama was completed in 1572. In the drama, which was written as a supplement to his kāvya, Kavikarṇapūra shows more mature judgement and fuller knowledge of the Master's life in Orissa. This drama is on the whole the most reliable account of Chaitanya as a monk. Kavikarṇapūra wrote also the *Gauraganoddeśa Dipikā*, based on mythology, in 1576.

A few Sanskrit poems of the followers of Chaitanya throw light on the last years of Chaitanya. Prabodhānanda Sarasvatī wrote a poem entitled *Chaitanya Chandrāmṛita,* consisting of 143 *ślokas* (verses). He describes the dance of Chaitanya in ecstasy in a flower garden on the sea coast and of his *darśan* (sight) of Jagannāth with tearful eyes. His work is one of the first to inculcate the worship of Chaitanya as the embodiment of Kṛishṇa. In the *Stavamālā* of Rūpa Gosvāmī, there are three *ashṭakas* (poems consisting of eight stanzas) in praise of Chaitanya. In his *Stavāvali* Raghunāth Dās Gosvāmī included two *stotras* (hymns) describing the love sickness of Chaitanya before his passing away. The

[2]Thus Viśvambhar cleaned a temple with shovel and broomstick (Murāri II.13.1-5). He toured in East Bengal to earn money (Murāri I.2.5). Chaitanya has been called 'Mahāpurusha' (Saint) in the *Chaitanya Chandrodaya* drama of Kavikarṇapūra (Canto IX). He sported in a tank at Puri and showed also acrobatic feats (The *Chaitanya Charitāmṛita kāvya* of Kavikarṇapūra, XVIII).

[3]'*The date of Chaitanya Charitāmrita of Murāri Gupta*': *Indian Historical Quarterly*, Vol. XX, pp. 132 ff.

first one is an *ashṭaka*. The second one in twelve ślokas or verses is called the *Gauraṅga Stavakalpataru.* From the Sanskrit source materials, we get furthermore an impression of the illustrious body of the Master.[4]

The Bengali Biographies of Chaitanya

The Bengali biographies were written for the masses and were embellished with fictitious and supernatural stories, because the importance of Navadvīpa declined when Chaitanya left the place for good in April 1510. Some contemporary poets wrote *padas* or devotional poems on Chaitanya's life. It is stated in their poems that Viśvambhar was imbued with the feeling of Kṛishṇa during the period of little more than one year at Navadvīpa before he became a Sannyāsī. Viśvambhar elaborately dressed himself as Krishna and imitated the erotic dalliance of Krishna with some of his companions dressed as Rādhā, Madhumati etc. But Murāri, who is more reliable, states that Viśvambhar spent his last days at Navadvīpa in a mood of spiritual absorption, constantly chanting the names Govinda and Krishna.[5] These *padas* created a lasting impression upon the followers of Chaitanya in Bengal.

Chaitanya was an ascetic with shaven head. He wore the scanty robes of a Sannyāsī.[6] But in his images and pictures he is shown as a well-dressed person with long locks of hair, to match with the picture and image of Nityānanda. The images and pictures show Viśvambhar and not Chaitanya.

1. *Chaitanya Bhāgavat*—The first biography of Chaitanya in Bengali was written by Vṛindāvan Dās in about 1550. As the work was intended for the masses, Vṛindāvan Dās added details from his imagination. It is stated in the *Chaitanya Bhāgavat* (I.9) that Sarasvatī, the goddess of learning, told a scholar in dream, not to challenge Viśvambhar in a disputation. The scholar admitted defeat and went away. Murāri writes that Hari (Viśvambhar) redeemed the *Mlechhas* (Muslims) during his *kirtana*

---

[4]Chaitanya's complexion surpassed even the dazzling glitter of gold (Rūpa's *Chaitanyāshṭaka* III.4). His was a tall and lustrous figure (*dirghojvala tanu*)—6th stanza of Raghunāth Das's *Chaitanyāshṭaka.* His arms stretched up to the thighs (*drāghimoddāma vāhu—Chaitanya Chandrodaya* drama IX.20)—Such a person spent about eighteen years at Puri in constant adoration of Krishna in a cell with little light and ventilation!

[5]Murāri II.12. 25-26.

[6]Raghunāth Dās writes in the *Stavakalpataru* that Chaitanya wore a loin cloth (*kaupīna*) which was covered by an outer garment (*bahirbāsa*) of ochre colour. A popular ballad in Bengali describes Chaitanya—'His head shaven, a torn rag on his back and a *karanka* (water pot made of a cocoanut shell) in his hand'!

processions.[7] Vṛindāvan Dās's story of the raid of the house of the Kāzi (Muslim Judge or city-Magistrate) of Navadvīpa by Viśvambhar at the head of a procession, is based on this slender information. Viśvambhar threatens to kill the Kāzi and to set fire to his house for stopping the *kirtana* processions.[8] Kavikarṇapūra, however, does not refer to this incident.

The *Chaitanya Bhāgavat* was written with the motive of describing Chaitanya as Krishna and Nityānanda as Kṛishṇa's elder brother Balarāma.[9] Vṛindāvan Dās succeeded in his mission. Chaitanya was worshipped in his lifetime by some devotees in Bengal as Krishna who was born at Navadvīpa in the Kaliyuga, whereas Balarāma was born as Nityānanda. But Nityānanda's abandonment of ascetic life was disliked by the orthodox Vaishṇavas in Bengal.[10]

The people had prejudice against apostasy.[11] It goes therefore to the credit of Vṛindāvan Dās that the publicity given in his book to the divinity of Nityānanda, lifted that religious teacher to a status next only to that of Chaitanya.[12] While Jñānadeva was ostracized, Nityānanda's son Vīrabhadra headed the Vaishṇava community in Bengal. Vṛindāvan Dās describes in detail the period when Nityānanda was closely associated with Chaitanya. The narration of the last phase of Chaitanya's life is consequently meagre.

2. *Chaitanya Charitāmṛita*—We will refer to this work, though

---

[7]*Kāvya* II.17.11

[8]*Chaitanya Bhāgavat* II.13.183. As the story depicts Viśvambhar in violent temper, Krishṇadās in his version of the incident tones it down (Ch. Ch. I.17. 136-40).

Vṛindavān Dās utilized another brief reference from Murāri Gupta, who writes that the Lord delivered from sin two wicked persons Jagannāth and Mādhava (*Kāvya* II.13.17). Kavikarṇapūra is silent about this incident. Vṛindāvan Dās writes that Mādhāi (Mādhava) hit Nityānanda's forehead with a potsherd which caused profused bleeding. But Nityānanda excused Mādhāi, which made the two sinners repent (*Chaitanya Bhāgavat* II.13). Kṛishṇadās Kavirāj makes no reference to the role of Nityānanda in the salvation of Jagāi (Jagannāth) and Mādhāi.

[9]But Murāri (*kāvya* II.14. 1-25) and Kavikarṇapūra (*kāvya*, VIII.19-50: drama Act II) refer to the Balabhadra feeling (*āveśa*) of Viśvāmbhar at Navadvīpa.

[10]*Chaitanya Bhāgavat* I.6.69; II.9 227; II.13.249. Vṛindāvan Dās threatens to kick these persons on their heads (*Ch. Bhāgavat* III.3).

[11]The father of saint Jñānadeva in the 13th century became a sannyāsī after his marriage. He again became a householder. "His children including Jñānadeva had to suffer from social obloquy", Majumdar, A.K., *Chaitanya, His Life and Doctrine*, p. 259.

[12]Vṛindāvan Dās's mother Nārāyaṇi became widow at the age of four. Vṛindāvan Dās was her illegitimate son. Nārāyaṇī and Vṛindāvān Dās in his boyhood suffered from social boycott. Nityānanda who had no social prejudice loved the boy Vṛindāvan Dās. Vṛindāvan Dās gratefully remembered the kindness of Nityānanda, who became his spiritual mentor, and exalted him in the *Chaitanya Bhāgavat*.

Jayānanda and Lochan Dās wrote lives of the Master before Kṛishṇadās Kavirāj. Half a century after the composition of the *Chaitanya Bhāgavat*, Kṛishṇadās was commissioned by the Gosvāmīs of Vṛindāvan to challenge the Navadvīpiya theory which was so ably expounded in the *Chaitanya Bhāgavat*. Though Kṛishṇadās Kavirāj was an erudite scholar in Sanskrit, he wrote the life of the Master in the language of the masses of Bengal. B.B. Majumdar has shown that *the Chaitanya Charitāmṛita* was completed in 1612 at Vṛindāvan. Some scholars hold the opinion that the *Charitāmṛita* was written in the last decade of the 16th century which appears to be purely conjectural. In this work especially Chaitanya's life after his initiation as a monk has been elaborately treated.

Dr. S.K. De writes "it is a profoundly laborious and learned work and is by far the most authoritative biography of Chaitanya."[13] He also observes: "It is a remarkable medieval document of mature theological scholarship which is by no means easy or elegant to read and which perhaps presents Chaitanya and his simple impassioned faith in a distorted perspective; but from the specialist point of view it is a work of rare merit."

Kṛishṇadās Kavirāj had the weakness of quoting appropriate *ślokas* for elaboration of the contexts without bothering about the sequence of events. Thus, as *tathāhi* (further reference), references were made from Rūpa Gosvāmī's *Bhaktirasāmṛita Sindhu* during Chaitanya's argumentation with Sārvabhauma. Referring to Chaitanya's argumentation with Rāmānanda, Dr. S.K. De writes: "The interlocutors quote and discuss with evident relish and precision of trained theologians, texts from the works of Rūpa, Sanātana, and Jiva and even from Kṛishṇadās's own *Govinda*

---

[13]S.K. De: *Early History of the Vaishnava Faith and Movement in Bengal*, p. 53.

Kṛishṇadās Kavirāj came to Vṛindāvan about 1557. He could have written an authoritative biography of Chaitanya by utilising the reminiscences of the three great Gosvāmīs Rūpa, Sanātana and Raghuñath Dās. Sanātana probably died in 1558. Kṛishṇadās did not try to obtain informations from Rūpa and Raghunāth Dās regarding the Master's life at Puri, as he decided to write a biography of Chaitanya in the second decade of the seventeenth century. By that time Rūpa Gosvāmī and Raghunāth Dās Gosvāmī had died. Rūpa Gosvāmī would not have told Kṛishṇadās Kavirāj that he read verses from Act V of his *Vidagdha Mādhava* drama, which he wrote in 1533, to Rāy Rāmānanda in 1516. Raghunāth Dās was closely associated with Rāy Rāmānanda and Svarūp Dāmodar at Puri. He would have told the biographer about Rāmānanda's discourses with Chaitanya at Rājamahendri, Kṛishṇadās Kavirāj made use of the slender informations which he got from *śloka* six of Rūpa Gosvāmī's *Chaitanyāshṭaka*, while writing chapter III.5. Similarly, he had followed Raghunāth Dās Gosvāmī's *Chaitanyāshṭaka* and *Stavakalpataru* while writing chapters III.17 and III.19. The last part of Kṛishṇadās Kavirāj's *Chaitanya Charitāmṛita*, is to a great extent, based on the kāvya and drama of Kavikarṇapūra, supplemented by his scholasticism and imagination.

Lilāmṛita, all of which had not yet been written."[14] These quotations were given by Kṛishṇadās Kavirāj to impart the authority of theology. He did not always adhere to sober history and facts were added from imagination. Chaitanya's journey in Karnataka and Maharashtra may be cited as an example. Kṛishṇadās furthermore has deliberately credited Chaitanya with stupendous knowledge in theology, who was capable of giving sixty-one interpretations to a verse of the *Bhāgavata* (I.7.10).[15] During Chaitanya's metaphysical discussion with Sārvabhauma, the exposition of Vedānta by that scholar in the drama of Kavikarṇapūra (Act VI) has been put in the mouth of Chaitanya by Kṛishṇadās.[16]

Like the *Chaitanya Bhāgavat*, the *Chaitanya Charitāmṛita* was written with a motive. The Gosvāmīs of Vṛindāvana, the seat of the exploits of Kṛishṇa, could not accept the theory of Kṛishṇa's manifestation at Navadvīpa. They attached more importance to the worship of Kṛishṇa and Rādhā than to the worship of Krishna and Balarāma. Lastly, they could not reconcile themselves to the idea that Kṛishṇa appeared as Chaitanya who was called Gaurāṅga for his very fair complexion.

Further, according to the Navadvīpa school, the worship of Chaitanya is the end in itself; while the Gosvāmīs preached that such a worship is the means to an end, which is the worship of Rādhā and Kṛishṇa. Kṛishṇadās Kavirāj quotes a verse in which Chaitanya has been described as Kṛishṇa who has incarnated again, possessing the spirit and complexion of Rādhā.[17] Rūpa Gosvāmī in the *Chaitanya Ashṭaka* in his *Stavamālā* writes that Kṛishṇa incarnated himself again, stealing the golden hue of Rādhā to conceal his dark complexion. In the first verse of the poem *Stavakalpataru* in the *Stavāvalī* by Raghunāth Dās Gosvāmī, there is an implication of the re-incarnation of Rādhā and Kṛishṇa in one indivisible body at Gauḍa.

In the *Chaitanya Charitāmṛita*, Kṛishṇadās expounded this new interpretation of the divinity of Chaitanya. He made Rāy Rāmānanda his

[14]De: Op. cit., p. 93. Dr. B.B. Majumdar similarly accuses Kṛishṇadās for putting in the mouth of Rāmānanda some ślokas, which he had not so far seen or were actually composed after his death. He writes: "Rāmānanda quoted from the *Brahma Samhita* and the *Govinda Lilamrita* (which Krishnadas wrote himself) during his discussion with Chaitanya."— *Chaitanya Chariter Upādān*, (C.C.U.) p. 356. (The name of this book will be abbreviated as C.C.U.). Rāmānanda recited two verses from the *Brahma Saṃhita* (*Ch. Ch.* II.8.29-30) and three verses from the *Govinda Lilāmrita* (*Ch. Ch.* II.8.40 and 44-45).

[15]*Ch. Ch.* II.24. But Murāri, who knew Viśvambhar as a student writes that his studies were confined to Sanskrit grammar and literature. (Murāri's kāvya I.15. 1-2).

[16]*C.C.U.*, p. 351.

[17]*Rādha-bhāva-dyuti subalita Kṛishṇa svarūpa.* This famous verse has been attributed to Sanātana Gosvāmī, by the commentator of the *Chaitanya Chandrāmṛita* (De: Op. cit., p. 433). In a spirit of compromise Kṛishṇadās also refers to Kṛishṇa's incarnation at Navadvīpa (*Ch. Ch.* I.3).

mouthpiece. In his narration of the theological discourses between Chaitanya and Rāmānanda, Kṛishṇadās put statements in the mouth of Rāmānanda to show that Chaitanya is the dual incarnation of Rādhā and Kṛishṇa.[18] Why did he consider Rāmānanda to be the suitable person? Even before he met Chaitanya, Rāmānanda had written a play entitled *Jagannāth Vallabha*, in which he narrated the dalliance of Kṛishṇa with Rādhā and the Gopīs. Sārvabhauma told the Master that Rāmānanda was a devout Vaishṇava.[19] Lastly, Chaitanya himself praised him. He told Sārvabhauma that he highly appreciated the doctrine (*mata*) of Rāmānanda.[20]

Two scholars have referred to the contribution of Rāmānanda to the theology of the Chaitanya faith. Dr. S.K. De writes: "After Chaitanya met Rāmānanda, the *Rādhābhāva* in Chaitanya became more intensified, as if Rāmānanda revealed him to himself."... "That the association with Rāmānanda apparently formed a turning point in Chaitanya's career of Bhakti is also indicated by the report of Kṛishṇadās, that it was the spiritual insight of Rāmānanda which revealed to Chaitanya that he had, for the purpose of realizing his own divine nature, usurped the complexion and spirit of Rādhā in the present *avatāra*."[21] A.K. Majumdar writes: "The identification of *Hlādini Śakti* (the counterpart) with Rādhā seems to be Rāmānanda's contribution to Gauḍīya Vaishṇavism."[22]

Kṛishṇadās Kavirāj utilized the *Ujjvala Nīlamaṇi* by Rūpa Gosvāmī, the *Prīti Sandarbha* and the *Kṛishṇa Sandarbha* by Jīva, for Rāmānanda's exposition of the Rādhā idea. These works were written long after the religious discourses at Rajamahendri, establishing the superiority of Rādhā over the Gopīs or milkmaids. In the *Chaitanya Charitāmṛita*, Rāmānanda told Chaitanya that Rādhā is the embodiment of *Mahābhāva* (the state of love in its fullest amplitude). This idea has been taken from the monograph *Prīti Sandarbha*. In the monograph, *Kṛishṇa Sandarbha*, Jīva explains that Rādhā alone, being the closest consort of Kṛishṇa, can attain *Mahābhāva*. The Gopīs cannot do so.

To justify his selection, Kṛishṇadās introduced two stories to show that Rāmānanda was a great scholar and a person of saintly character. The sources of these two stories are not known. Kṛishṇadās writes that Rāmānanda tested Rūpa's knowledge of Vaishṇava theology. Rūpa recited ślokas from his play, *Vidagdha Mādhava* for Rāmānanda's opinion. The *Vidagdha Mādhava* was written in 1533, but Rūpa quoted from the

---

[18]*Ch. Ch.*, II.8. 230.

[19]'Uttama Bhāgavata'.

Chaitanya Chandrodaya drama of Kavikarṇapūra, Canto IX.

[20]*Chaitanya Chandrodaya*, VI (See Chapter III, Footnote 38).

[21]De: op. cit, pp. 435-6.

[22]A.K. Majumdar: *Chaitanya: His Life and Doctrine*, p. 195.

fifth act of his play in 1516, when he met Rāmānanda.[23] It is stated by Kṛishṇadās that Rāmānanda gave training to two temple girls for the performance of his play *Jagannāth Vallabha.* He dressed and rubbed their bodies. When there was a complaint, Chaitanya defended Rāmānanda by declaring that of all persons, Rāmānanda alone was indifferent to carnal feelings. He would remain passionless, even when touching a woman, as if he had touched wood or a piece of stone. Even he himself, Chaitanya admitted, would be mentally perturbed at the sight of a woman.[24] Apart from the delicate question, whether it is necessary to massage the limbs of a young girl to teach her dancing and music, it is difficult to believe that Chaitanya approved this kind of teaching by Rāmānanda.[25]

Though he largely depended on the *kāvya* and drama of Kavikarṇapūra for materials relating to the theological dialogue between Chaitanya and Rāmānanda at Rajamahendri, Kṛishṇadās deliberately avoided acknowledgment to Kavikarṇapūra. It would have exposed the unauthenticity of the passages which Kṛishṇadās added to show that Chaitanya is the combined manifestation of Rādhā and Kṛishṇa. Instead of the works of Kavikarṇapūra, Kṛishṇadās refers to the *kaḍchā* (notes) of Svarūp Dāmodar as the source of his information for the narration of the dialogue at Rajamahendri.[26] He also writes that Svarūp Dāmodar has briefly described the last phase of Chaitanya's life in his 'note book' (*grantha*).[27] But Kṛishṇadās Kavirāj has not quoted a single line from the *kaḍchā* of Svarūp Dāmodar in the last part of his work.

It is held that the *kaḍchā* of Svarūp Dāmodar consists of biographical notes on Chaitanya, and it is now lost. The word *kaḍchā* also signifies the collection of verses composed by a person. Kṛishṇadās had used the word in the second sense while referring to Raghunāth Dās and other *kaḍchā*-writers.[28] Raghunāth Dās wrote only twenty ślokas in his *Stavāvalī.* But he is called a *kaḍchā*-writer. We presume that the *kaḍchā* of Svarūp Dāmodar consists of some verses which are quoted in the

[23]*C.C.U.*, p. 386.

[24]*Ch. Ch.* II.5.36. Kṛishṇadās Kavirāj like Vṛindāvan Dās, puts statements in the mouth of Chaitanya exonerating persons from blame. In the *Chaitanya Bhāgavat* (III.7.24) Chaitanya says that even if Nityānanda drinks wine and lives with a *Yavanī* (Muslim woman) he is revered by Brahmā himself. Chaitanya, a strict moralist, would not have made such a statement even in favour of Nityānanda.

[25]Chaitanya set up a high standard of morality even for the Vaishṇava householders during his instructions to Advaita (*Ch. Ch.* II.12. 90-100).

[26]*Ch. Ch.* II.8.261.

We are to believe that Svarūp Dāmodar, a close friend of Rāmānanda, heard the story from Rāmānanda himself.

[27]*Ch. Ch.* I.16.15.

[28]*Ch. Ch.* III.14.69.

Chaitanya Charitāmṛita and in Kavikarṇapūra's *Gaura Gaṇoddeśa Dīpikā*, long after the death of Svarūp Dāmodar.

Kṛishṇadās narrates an incident having a moral lesson, which does little credit to Chaitanya. He writes that young Haridās, a cenobite, was asked by his preceptor to meet Mādhavi Dāsī, an old anchoress. Chaitanya discarded young Haridās for the offence of talking with a woman (*prakriti sambhāsana*). Haridās committed suicide in shame. The example was not lost because the ascetic Vaishṇavas at Puri 'stopped talking with women even in their dreams'.[29] Kṛishṇadās Kavirāj writes in the same canto that Mādhavi Dāsī was considered to be a half 'Pātra' (favourite of Rādhā) for her piety and learning. In his book, there is reference to a beautiful prostitute who became a devout Vaishṇavī by listening to the chanting of the name of Hari by Yavana Haridās. "Prominent Vaishṇavas went to see her."[30] As he could not obtain sufficient materials for writing *antya līlā* (last part of Chaitanya's life) which was comparatively uneventful, the old pious Vaishṇava at Vṛindāvana penned down tales without proper scrutiny.

Kṛishṇadās Kavirāj wanted to show that Chaitanya is the manifestation of Kṛishṇa, with the spirit and complexion of Rādhā, and he was imbued with the feeling of Rādhā, in his last days, pining for Kṛishṇa. So Kṛishṇadās put in the mouth of Chaitanya many ślokas, which he composed for his *Govinda Līlāmṛita*.[31]

Kṛishṇadās Kavirāj has been criticized for his silence regarding Chaitanya's association with those Oriya Vaishṇavas who did not accept the tenets of the Chaitanya faith. The truth is that he wrote '*Charitāmṛita*' ("biography which is like nectar") for the devotees. Thousands of them have derived peace of mind and happiness by reading this book, without caring for historical truth.

3. *Chaitanya Maṅgal* by Jayānanda—Next in importance to the *Chaitanya Bhāgavat* and the *Chaitanya Charitāmṛita*, Jayānanda's work was written in about 1560. He composed poems to be sung by the common people. Later on, these poems were elaborated by stories based on hearsay. Some of the statements of Jayānanda are *prima facie* absurd. He writes that Chaitanya gave the garland on his neck to Chandrakalā, the chief consort of king Pratāpa Rudra, who had hundred wives. It is stated that Chaitanya sent Nityānanda to Puri, before he went there and that he rebuked Rāmānanda for his apathy to the worship of Kṛishṇa. Some verses in the '*Vijay khaṇḍa*', a part of the *Chaitanya Maṅgal*, credit Chaitanya with the role of a political adviser to Pratāpa Rudra. These verses are apparently interpolated (See chapter X).

---

[29]*Ch. Ch.* III.2.144.
[30]*Ch. Ch.* III.3.144.
[31]*C.C.U.*, p.392.

Nevertheless, Jayānanda's *Chaitanya Maṅgal* contains some statements which may be true. He writes that Chaitanya's ancestors lived at Jajpur in Orissa. He alone gives detailed information about the places which Chaitanya visited on his way to Puri.

4. *Chaitanya Maṅgal* by Lochan Dās—A decade after Jayānanda, Lochan Dās wrote another *Chaitanya Maṅgal.* For the source-materials he largely depended on Murāri Gupta's *Chaitanya Charitāmrita* which he acknowledged. In the third part of his work, Lochan Dās refers to Chaitanya's passing away in the Guṇḍichā House 'absorbing himself into the image of Jagannāth'.

Īśān Nāgar was an attendant of Advaita, a prominent associate of Chaitanya. In his *Advaita Prakās,* Īśan Nāgar describes Chaitanya's passing away in the Jagannāth temple. Another work mentioning Chaitanya is Narahari Chakravarti's *Bhakti Ratnākar.* It was written in the beginning of the eighteenth century. Only incidentally it refers to the last phase of Chaitanya's life.

The principal Sanskrit and Bengali biographies of Chaitanya have a distinct advantage over the Oriya literary sources of Chaitanya's life. As stated earlier, the three Sanskrit works were written by persons who knew Chaitanya. Vṛindāvan Dās consulted Nityānanda, one of the closest followers of Chaitanya while writing the biography of Chaitanya. Kānāi Khuntia and Achyutānanda, two Oriya followers of Chaitanya, made only incidental references to the Master in their writings.

CHAPTER II

Chaitanya in Oriya Literature

THE ORIYA literary sources supplement our knowledge of the Chaitanya period in Orissa. We learn from these sources that Chaitanya had a large number of followers, headed by Jagannātha Dāsa, Balarāma, Achyutānanda, Yaśovanta and Ananta who were called *Pañcha Sakhā* ("five comrades"). That Chaitanya passed away before the image of Jagannāth; and that Chaitanya was also considered to be Buddha-Jagannāth.

(1) *ŚŪNYA SAṂHITĀ by* ACHYUTANANDA

Achyutānanda incidentally refers to Chaitanya in his *Śūnya-Saṃhitā*, which is a masterpiece of esoteric Vaishṇava literature. In the *Śūnya Saṃhitā*, Achyutānanda attempted to synthesize the concept of Buddha-Jagannāth with that of Chaitanya. The *Śūnya Saṃhitā* was probably written during the reign of king Mukundadeva (1560-1568) whose son-in-law was Achyutānanda's patron.

Achyutānanda was an eye-witness of the passing away of Chaitanya. The Master has been deified in the *Śūnya Saṃhitā* by Achyutānanda who writes: "Chaitanya, the Master is the Lord Himself."[1] 'He has appeared to redeem the sinners.'[2]

Achyutānanda writes that he participated in the *kirtana* processions of Gaurāṅga Chandra, along with his comrades Ananta, Yaśovanta, Balarāma, and Jagannātha.[3] According to his narration, he was the first to receive the grace of Chaitanya. "Then Ananta, Yaśovanta, Balarāma, Śrīvatsa alias Jagannātha Dāsa also participated. Thus were all the five comrades present and by the order of Chaitanya, the chanting of the name

---

[1] *Śrī Chaitanya Prabhu āpe Jagata thākura—Śūnya Saṃhitā*, X.

[2] *Nāma Śrī Chaitanya Prabhu adhama uddhāra—Śūnya Saṃhitā*, III.

[3] *Ananta Achyuta gheni Yaśovanta Balarāma Jagannātha*
E Pañcha Sakhāhni nṛutya kari gale Gaurānga Chandra sangata
Śūnya Saṃhitā, I.

of Hari from every house rent the air."[4] "The *Śūnya Saṃhitā* makes no reference to the prominent followers of Chaitanya such as Nityānanda, Rāmānanda and Svarūp Dāmodar.

(2) *MAHĀBHĀVA PRAKAŚA* by KANHEI (KANAI) KHUNTIA

Kanhei Khuntia was a servitor of the Jagannāth temple. The last part of his work, the *Mahābhāva Prakāśa* is lost. Only the first two cantos and a portion of the third have been published. The work deals with the idea (*tattva*) of Rādhā which the writer had heard from Chaitanya himself.[5] The Master explains to Kanhei Khuntia that Rādhā is the embodiment of *Mahābhāva* or supreme bliss.

The work refers to Keśava Bhārati and Mādhavendra Purī, who are called devout Vaishṇavas. It corroborates the statement in the *Chaitanya Charitāmṛita* that Rāy Rāmānanda was devoted to Kṛishṇa and could not properly manage the affairs of the province of Rajamahendri (canto 2). Kanhei vividly describes the *bhāvāveśa* (emotional ecstasy) of Chaitanya at the sight of Jagannāth. He once noticed that the effulgence from the eyes of Jagannāth fell upon the face of Chaitanya! He refers to Svarūp Dāmodar and to Govinda. He praises the king of Orissa for his devotion to the Master. Kanhei writes that Chaitanya, after taking sannyāsa, reached Puri in the year 918 (*Naasa athara sāle prabeśa hoilā*). The Umlee (islamic) year 918 has been obviously interpolated after the Muslim conquest of Orissa. Kanhei is silent about Kāsī Miśra, Tulasi Parichha and other attendants of the Jagannāth temple. Historically, the importance of the work lies in the description of the Muslim invasion of Orissa in 1511 A.D.

(3) *CHAITANYA VILĀSA* by MADHAVA DASA

B.B. Majumdar first traced a copy of this manuscript. He attributes the authorship to Mādhava Patnaik, who has been mentioned in the *Vaishṇava Vandanā* works as a pious Vaishṇava. In his opinion, Lochan Dās has followed Mādhava while narrating the sannyāsa of Chaitanya.[6] There is not sufficient evidence to justify such an inference. To justify this it has to be established that this Oriya manuscript reached Lochan Dās before

---

[4]*Ananta ye Yaśovanta Balarāma Śrīvatsa milile āsi*
Jagannātha Dāsa gheni Pañcha Sakhā udaya hoile tahni
Ghare ghare Hari dhani uchhulilā, Chaitanya ājñā pāi
Śūnya Samhitā, I.

[5]*Yāhā mñu Guru Gaurānga mukharu śunili Sehi Mahābhāva muhñi mātra Ye lekhili. Mahābhāva Prakāśa*: Canto II.

[6]*C.C.U.*, p. 283.

1566 and he considered it important for narrating the incidents which took place in Bengal. No contemporary writer, Oriya or Bengali, refers to the *Chaitanya Vilāsa.* On the contrary Mādhava himself admits that he has translated into Oriya language, what 'Thākur' has said.[7] It appears that a portion of the *Chaitanya Vilāsa* is based on the *Chaitanya Maṅgal* by Lochan Dās, who respectfully addresses his preceptor Narahari Sarkar as 'Thākur' (spiritual guide).

(4) *MAYURA CHANDRIKĀ by* Sri Hari Dasa

The writer probably flourished towards the end of the 16th century. He calls Rāy Rāmānanda as his preceptor and refers to Rāmānanda's religious discourse with Chaitanya[8] whom he invokes as Kṛishṇa Chaitanya (canto 6). The poet writes that Chaitanya has manifested himself at Nadia, concealing his (dark) complexion (canto 14). He refers to Gaurāṅga's contemplation of Rādhā and Kṛishṇa with tearful eyes (canto 1). Śrī Hari Dāsa makes obeisance to Advaita and Nityānanda in the beginning of the poem. He writes that Rādhā and Kṛishṇa are manifest in Jagannāth (canto 12).

(5) *CHAITANYA BHĀGAVATA by* Isvara Dasa

The *Chaitanya Bhāgavata* was probably written in the second half of the seventeenth century.[9] The author writes that at the time of the completion of the work, Chaitanya's passing away was still talked about. When he showed his manuscript in the Mukti Maṇḍapa of the Jagannāth temple, Vāsudeva Tīrtha, a sannyāsī, expressed his doubt about Chaitanya's merger into Jagannāth. Īśvara Dāsa, like Achyutānanda, describes Chaitanya as the embodiment of Buddha-Jagannāth.

"The poet's source of the book has been mainly stories and names collected from traditional hearsay. . . . The book is more a devotional account than real history. Sri Chaitanya perhaps became a legend when the poet came to the field."[10] Īśvara Dāsa's account suffers from extreme credulity for all miraculous legends relating to Chaitanya. The work, being a *Bhāgavata,* is written in the form of a dialogue between the sage Agastya and an unnamed king of Sampurṇa Nagara. The writer borrows the character, sage Agastya, from Śāraḷā Dāsa's *Mahābhārata,* where he

---

[7](X. 17) *Chaitanya Vilāsa.*

[8]*Kahanti Gurudeva Rāy Rāmānanda.*
Śunanti ānande Śachī suta Gorāchānda,
Mayura Chandrikā, canto 2.

[9]The *Chaitanya Bhāgavata* refers to Vīrabhadra, son of Nityānanda (canto 64). In Īśvara Dāsa's time, the conception of Buddha-Jagannāth had not lost popularity.

[10]C.R. Das—*Medieval Religion and Literature in Orissa,* p. 34.

is a story-teller to Vaivasvata Manu. By the time the work was written, the deification of Chaitanya was firmly established in Orissa. In the Dvāpara Yuga, Devakī bore Kṛishṇa in her womb, but could not bring him up. Śachī, the mother of Chaitanya, dreamt that Jagannāth came into her womb in the form of Kṛishṇa (canto I).

Īśvara Dāsa's *Chaitanya Bhāgavata* has a distinct value. Behind a mass of facts, loosely arranged and at times incredible, we glean valuable informations regarding the history of Vaishṇavism and allied sects in Orissa. Īśvara introduced a large number of persons in his work, without caring for historical sequence. Nānak, Kabir, Buddhist Vīrasiṃha, Vīrabhadra, Jaṅgali, Nandini, Jagāi, Mādhāi are all introduced indiscriminately.

Īśvara Dāsa's *Chaitanya Bhāgavata* is an important contribution to Oriya Vaishṇava literature for the following reasons: Firstly, Īśvara writes that Chaitanya is the embodiment of Jagannāth.[11] The Puri deity has been identified with the ninth incarnation of the Lord (Bhagavān) who says that in that incarnation He will embody compassion and talk of enlightenment. So He will be known as Bodhāvatara. Secondly, Īśvara gives a detailed description of Chaitanya's association with 'five comrades' (*Pañcha Sakhā*). Thirdly, Īśvara is the only writer who rises above sectarian feelings. In his *Chaitanya Bhāgavata*, the Gauḍīya Vaishṇavas and five comrades mix freely and participate in the *kirtana* processions led by the Master.[12] To this extent Īśvara Dāsa alone states historical fact. Lastly, by the time the *Chaitanya Bhāgavata* was written, Nityānanda had been identified with Balarāma. In canto 2, Vishṇu (Kṛishṇa) says to Nārada that he would be born at Nadia for the salvation of mankind. Balabhadra would be born as Nityānanda. In canto 47, it is again stated that Nityānanda is the embodiment of Saṅkarshaṇa.

In canto 46, Rāma Rāy meets Chaitanya at Navadvīpa and has religious discussion with him. Because he gave *ānanda* (joy) to Chaitanya, the Master named him Rāmānanda. In the same canto, Īśvara Dāsa describes Chaitanya's journey to Orissa. After bathing in the Vaitarani river, Chaitanya visited the temple of Ādivarāha. After spending a night at the outskirts of Cuttack, he continued his journey. He bathed in the river Kusabhadra, which is stated to be as sacred as the Gangā. Thence he proceeded to Bhubaneswar and visited the Śiva temples. From Bhubneswar, he proceeded to Konarka. On his way, he worshipped twelve Śiva liṅgas near the mouth of the river Prāchi.

---

[11]*Chaitanya rūpa Jagannātha*—canto p. 47.

[12]One *kirtana* party was attended by Uddatta (Uddhārana Dutta), Aditya (Advaita), Vakreśvar, Gauridās, Sundarānanda and the five comrades. In another *kirtana* party shortly before Chaitanya's passing away, Śrīvās, Sārvabhauma, Gauridās, Gadādhar and the five comrades were present.

In canto 47, Īśvara Dāsa describes Chaitanya's first visit to the Jagannāth temple, accompanied by Advaita, Vāsudeva, Sārvabhauma, and Rāmānanda.

In canto 49, king Pratāpa Rudra comes with a large retinue to Puri. He visited the Jagannāth temple. He heard an oracle "Listen, O king. Fall at the feet of Chaitanya and take the great mantra from him." The king accordingly met the Master. "Chaitanya, the Lord Himself" (*Chaitanya āpe Bhagavāna*) embraced the king and imparted the mantra. But suddenly an elephant ran amuck. Balarāma Dāsa chanted the names of Hari into the ears of the mad elephant. It became pacified and bowed at the feet of Chaitanya, who addressed Balarāma as 'Matta' Balarāma. The king presented the elephant to Chaitanya, who was at first unwilling to take the elephant, he being an ascetic.

(6) *JAGANNĀTHA CHARITĀMṚITA by* DIVAKARA DASA

Divākara wrote the biography of Jagannātha Dāsa—one of the five comrades. It is the first biographical work in Oriya literature. He belonged to the 'Ati Baḍi' sect founded by Jagannātha Dāsa and was the fifth in preceptorial descent from him. It is generally held that he lived in the middle of the seventeenth century.

Divākara writes that Jagannātha Dāsa first met the Master at the age of eighteen. He was at that time reciting from the *Bhāgavata* under the banyan tree within the Jagannāth temple precincts. Chaitanya used to come to the temple for the sight of Jagannāth every day. He listened to the exposition of the (*Bhāgavata*) Purāṇa and stayed there with overflowing love.[13] For eight years, Jagannātha constantly served Chaitanya.[14]

The first seven cantos of the *Jagannātha Charitāmrita* refer to Chaitanya's life in Orissa. He asks Balarāma Dāsa to initiate Jagannātha Dāsa (canto 2). Accompanied by Jagannāth Dāsa, Chaitanya goes to the house of Sārvabhauma and learns from him the principles (*tattva*) of Jagannāth worship (canto 4). Chaitanya explains the implications of 'Hare Rāma Kṛishṇa' *mantra* to Nityānanda in the presence of Jagannātha Dāsa and other Vaishṇavas. He explains '*Prema Pañchātmaka*' (five modes of love) to the Vaishṇavas (canto 6). Pratāpa Rudra pays homage to Chaitanya and arranges his accommodation in the Vakula Maṭh (canto 7). Chaitanya's disappearance is also described in this canto.

Like the *Chaitanya Charitāmṛita* of Kṛishṇadās Kavirāj, the

---

[13] *Prati dibase Chaitanya* *Āsanti kari darśana*
Baṭa tale Purāṇa śuṇi *Daṇḍe rahanti preme puṇi*
Jagannātha Charitāmṛita—canto 2.

[14] *Ashṭa varasha nirantara* *Sebile Chaitanya payara*",
Jagannātha Charitāmṛita—canto 2.

Jagannātha Charitāmṛita was written for the glorification of a sect. While Kṛishṇadās utilized the source-materials on Chaitanya's life, Divākara's references to Chaitanya are based on stories, legends and on his own imagination.[15] Divākara knew Sanskrit well and quoted a large number of *ślokas* in his work. But he did not consult the Sanskrit biographies of Chaitanya written by Murāri Gupta and Kavikarṇapūra.

Divākara writes that one day Chaitanya asked Jagannātha about his past birth. With humility, Jagannātha replied: "Suffer me to recount the facts, O Master, which are known to you. Once a while I was meditating on Rādhā and Kṛishṇa, I could realize that Rādhā and Kṛishṇa were gazing coyly at each other's face. From the laugh of Kṛishṇa, you were born. Rādhā smiled prettily and from that laugh, I was born. You have appeared in the Kaliyuga for the salvation of the sinners." Chaitanya exclaimed: "You are then a partial manifestation of Śrī Rādhā—the supreme object of Kṛishṇa's love! Only the adepts are able to comprehend the mellowness of Rādhā's love. In sooth, you are a great person. Then taking off, his red-ochred wrapper, he tied it round the head of Jagannātha and said: 'You have spoken great words. So you shall be known as very great (*ati baḍa*)."[16]

The matter did not end there. Divākara writes that the Gauḍīya Vaishṇavas became jealous of Chaitanya's intimacy with Jagannātha Dāsa. They told Chaitanya "O Master, let us not stay only in one kingdom. We should visit other holy places such as Gayā and bathe in the mouth of the Gaṅgā." But Chaitanya turned down their suggestion and refused to leave Jagannāth Kshetra. At this flat refusal, the Gauḍīya Vaishṇavas decided to abandon the Master. They blamed Chaitanya for his close contact with the Oriya Vaishṇavas. Out of spite, they decided to go away to Vṛindāvana. On their way, they halted at Jājpur. Chaitanya sent a messenger to persuade them to come back to Puri. But they refused and made their way to Vṛindāvana. They used to come to Puri during the chariot festivals. But the Master's partiality for Jagannātha Dāsa made them hasten their departure.

Divākara Dāsa's statement is highly embellished, motivated by sectarian differences. Divākara did not cite the source, on which he based his accusation against the Gauḍīya Vaishṇavas. There is no doubt that Chaitanya honoured the translator of the *Bhāgavata* with the title of

---

[15]Chaitanya's grandfather Vishṇu Paṇḍa named him Chaitanya after his birth! Divākara describes Jība(n) Gosvāmī as one of the followers of Chaitanya. It is stated that after taking *sannyāsa*, Chaitanya visited many places including Vṛindāvana, but nowhere he found *Prema Bhakti* (devotion based on love). So he came to Purushottama Kshetra and settled there (canto 2).

[16]*Ati baḍa kathā kahile tenu atibaḍa hele*

Jagannātha Charitāmṛita—canto 3.

Ati Baḍa for his erudition and it appears that some Gauḍīya Vaishṇavas became jealous. But reliable evidence is necessary to corroborate the fact that the Gauḍīya Vaishṇavas left Puri for Vṛindāvana and defied the request of Chaitanya to come back to Puri. Few Gauḍīya Vaishṇavas had settled at Vṛindāvana during the lifetime of Chaitanya. It is curious that the *Jagannātha Charitāmṛita* shows the influence of the Chaitanya faith, which it tries to discredit.[17]

Divākara refers to a table of preceptorial descent in canto 7 of his work. Chaitanya is stated to be the preceptor of Gaurīdās Paṇḍit, who was believed to be an embodiment of Chaitanya-Nityānanda. Hṛidayānanda was the disciple of Gaurīdās.[18] He was the spiritual guide of Balarāma Dāsa. Though a non-Brahman, Balarāma was made the preceptor of Jagannātha Dāsa, one of the greatest Brahmans of Orissa.

(7) *YAŚOVANTA DĀSAṄKA CHAURĀŚI ĀJÑĀ*[19] *by* SUDARSANA DASA

This unpublished manuscript was probably written towards the end of the seventeenth century. There is reference to Sālabeg, who became a disciple of Yaśovanta. Sālabeg, a Muslim Vaishṇava poet, lived in the middle of the seventeenth century at Puri. Thus Yaśovanta of the sixteenth century cannot be his preceptor. The *Chaurāśi Ājñā*, contains a number of miracles to show the occult power of Yaśovanta. It also refers to Chaitanya's association with Yaśovanta and four other comrades.

(8) *EIGHTEENTH CENTURY WORKS*

Towards the end of the eighteenth century, Sadānanda Kavisūrya

[17]Divākara Dāsa describes Jagannātha Dāsa as an embodiment of Rādhā. It is stated that Jagannātha used to put on female dress to imitate the feeling of Rādhā. But Jagannātha does not refer to Rādhā in his translation of the *Bhāgavata*. According to the Chaitanya faith, Gadādhar Paṇḍit is the embodiment of Rādhā. He used to dress as Rādhā. This fact has been stated by Iśvara Dāsa in his *Chaitanya Bhāgavata*, canto 62. Gadādhar spent his last years at Puri.

Divākara writes that Jagannātha once physically became a woman by his occult power. There is a similar story about Nandini and Jaṅgali. They were male disciples of Sītā, wife of Advaita. They dressed and lived like women to imbue the feeling of the Gopīs. Iśvara Dāsa refers to them in his *Chaitanya Bhāgavata*, canto 64. Nandini settled at Puri to worship Gopīnāth. He died there.

[18]The table of preceptorial descent is also mentioned in the *Nityaguptamaṇi* (Canto 19), a Sanskrit work, which is ascribed to Divākara Dāsa. Hṛidayānanda was a nephew of Gadādhar Paṇḍit. He lived for some time at Puri. Then he went to Kālnā near Śāntipur in Bengal and became the pupil of Gauridās Paṇḍit. Hṛidāyananda was also the preceptor of Śyāmānanda.

[19]Eighty-four is a conventional number. At Balarāma Dāsa's command, an idiot expounded eighty-four *mantras* (*Vedānta sāra*, *Gupta Gītā*, I).

Brahmā delineated the Chaitanya faith in his writings. In the *Prema Tarāṅgiṇī*, he describes the glory of the 'Gaurā-Avatāra'. He writes that Kṛishṇa incarnated himself to be Rādhā and Kṛishṇa in one body.[20]

In the *Nisṭhā Nilamaṇi* (canto 3) he makes it clear that devotion to Gaurāṅga is fruitless without the grace of Gadādhar Paṇḍit, from whom he traces his preceptorial descent. In the *Viśvambhara Vihāra*, the early life of Chaitanya has been described.

In the eighteenth century, Rājā Govinda Bhañja of Keonjhar composed the *Charaṇa Sudhānidhi*. He reveres Chaitanya as an incarnation of Kṛishṇa.[21]

Bhagavān Dāsa wrote the *Gaurāṇga Bhāgavata* describing the last years of Chaitanya's life when he was love sick. It is a free translation of the *Chaitanya Charitāmṛita*. The author is likely to be Bhagavāna Dāsa who lived at Puri in the middle of the eighteenth century and became the Mahant of Gaṅgāmātā Maṭh. He uses the obsolete word 'Chaḍeiāgiri' instead of Chatak hill. His Guru was Govindadeva, the author of the *Gaura-Krishnodaya kāvya* in Sanskrit, which was written in 1680 Śaka (1758 A.D.). This Kāvya is based on the *Chaitanya Charitāmṛita*. Furthermore, B. B. Majumdar refers to *Śrī Chaitanya-Sārvabhauma Saṁvāda* and places it in the eighteenth century.[22] The writer tries to make a synthesis between the principle of Void and the Chaitanya faith. Chaitanya explains Śūnya Brahma to Sārvabhauma.

(9) *NINETEENTH CENTURY WORKS*

In the nineteenth century, the following manuscripts were written by the devotees. Historically, these works are not important.

1. *Sri Chaitanya Gītā* . . Bhramaravara Das
2. *Chaitanyāvali* . . Govinda Bhatta
3. *Manasikshā* . . Bhaktacharan Das
4. *Chaitanya Pañchaka* . . Bisvanāth Deo, Rāja of Athgarh.

---

[20] *Kṛishṇa Chaitanya rūpe avatāri ye Rādhā-Kṛishṇa eka dehare bhajile*
Prema Tarāṅginī

[21] *Chaitanyāvatāre prema bhakta hoi Gaurahari rūpa jagate dekhāi*
Charaṇa Sudhā Nidhi.

[22] *C.C.U.*, p. 495.

CHAPTER III

Chaitanya in Orissa

CHAITANYA'S EARLY name before his initiation into the monastic order was Viśvāmbhar. He was born at Navadvīpa on 27 February 1486—Phālguna Purṇima, Śaka 1407. His father Jagannāth Miśra was inclined towards Vaishṇavism. There was a small Vaishṇava community at Navadvīpa, headed by a venerable old man named Advaita.

Viśvāmbhar, after the death of his father, became a householder. He started a Sanskrit school for imparting scholastic education. His future preceptor Īśvara Puri once came to Navadvīpa and met Viśvāmbhar in his house.[1] During his absence on tour in Bengal to earn money, his wife Lakshmī died. To please his mother Śachī, Viśvāmbhar married again. But Vishṇupriyā, the second wife, could not fill the void of his heart, made by the sudden death of Lakshmī. It appears that Viśvāmbhar sought solace from religious discussion with Īśvara Puri, when he went to Gayā.

Up to the age of twenty, Viśvāmbhar evinced little interest in religion. It seemed that he would spend his life as a householder and a school master. But suddenly, a great change took place in his life, which completely changed its course.

(i) Beginning of Spiritual Disposition

Towards the end of 1508, at the age of twenty-two, the Viśvāmbhar went to Gayā to offer oblations to the departed soul of his father. It so happened that Īśvara Puri, whom he had met at Navadvīpa, was also staying at Gayā at that time.[2] Īśvara Puri and Viśvāmbhar had long

[1]It is said that the young scholar pointed out grammatical mistakes in Īśvara Puri's work on Kṛishṇa worship, which he showed to Viśvāmbhar for his opinion. The Vaishṇava community at Navadvipa was sorry that Viśvāmbhar had no liking for Kṛishṇa worship (*Chaitanya Bhāgavat* I.8.83).

[2]Īśvara Puri belonged to the Puri order of the Advaitic school of Śaṅkara. The orthodox monks were required to conform to one of the ten orders founded by

religious discourses on Kṛishṇa, which made lasting impression upon Viśvāmbhar's mind. He thought he had found out the truth. Īśvara Puri imparted to him *mantra* (esoteric knowledge) for worshipping Gopāla (Kṛishṇa). The discussion with Īśvara Puri shaped the spiritual disposition of Viśvambhar. He was completely a changed man, when he returned to Navadvīpa in January 1510.

(ii) Last days at Navadvīpa

Viśvāmbhar became an ardent devotee of Kṛishṇa. Though he maintained his school for four more months, he lost all interest in teaching.[3] He experienced devotional ecstasy, while constantly chanting the names Govinda, Kṛishṇa.[4] He spent his time in the company of Murāri, Advaita, Gadādhar, Śrīvās, and other Vaishṇavas at Navadvīpa. Nityānanda, a monk from his boyhood, came to Navadvīpa and soon became the most prominent disciple of Viśvambhar.

Kirtana processions were now organized under the leadership of Viśvāmbhar. A large number of persons, who had remained so far indifferent, took part in the *kirtana* processions with musical instruments. It is stated in the Bengali biographies of Chaitanya that the Kāzi (Muslim city Magistrate) of Navadvīpa forcibly stopped *Nagara-kirtana* (street singing) which he considered to be public demonstration of idol worship. Viśvambhar was angry when the news reached him. He organized a mass rally and led a procession to the Kāzi's house. The Kāzi was frightened and promised to allow *Nagara-kirtana* in future without any interference.

It may be a fact that this incident of demonstration against the Kāzi influenced Viśvāmbhar's decision to renounce the world. He realized that it would not be possible to give up passions so long he was tied with the worldly affairs. But the chief motive for his adoption of asceticism seems to be the desire to surrender himself fully to the service of Kṛishṇa. He resolved to give up the life of a householder which distracted his attention from Kṛishṇa.[5] Sannyāsa or renunciation of the world

---

Śaṅkara, such as Purī, Aranaya, and Bhārati. Īśvara Puri and his preceptor Mādhavendra Puri were inclined towards emotional devotion, though they belonged to a Śaṅkarite order. Mādhavendra Puri is said to have introduced a *mantra,* consisting of ten letters, for the worship of Gopāla Kṛishṇa. He lived at Vṛindāvana. "It is sufficient to assume the period from c.A.D. 1420 to 1490 to be roughly his lifetime". Dr. F. Hardy: 'Mādhavendra Purī: A link between Bengal Vaishṇavism and South Indian *Bhakti': Journal of Royal Asiatic Society*, 1974, p. 31.

[3]A. Kavikarṇapūra's *kāvya*, V. 24.

[4]*Murāri* II. 12.25-26.

[5]Chaitanya told Sārvabhauma at Puri: "Pining after Kṛishṇa, I shaved my head and became a monk", *Ch. Bhāgavat* III.3.62.

is an ancient Indian ideal. Viśvambhar might have become an *Avadhuta* Sannyāsī, for which no initiation was necessary. But the ordained monks were more respected. Viśvambhar fixed an auspicious hour for taking up asceticism. At that time, Keśava, Bhārati, a monk of the Bhārati order of Śaṅkara, was staying at Katwa, 24 miles away from Navadvīpa. Viśvāmbhar went there to take initiation (*dikshā*) from Keśava Bhārati.[6]

On 23 January 1510, at the age of 24, Viśvāmbhar was ordained as a monk by Keśava Bhārati. Viśvāmbhar requested Keśava Bhārati to initiate him by a new mantra, which he himself suggested.[7] After initiation, Keśava Bhārati named him Śrī Kṛishṇa Chaitanya.[8] Later, the new Sannyāsī came to be known by his Śaṅkarite title of Chaitanya.[9] But he did not take the final vows of the Bhārati order.[10]

Immediately after his initiation as a monk, Chaitanya went to Rāmeśvaram. It appears that he went there to visit the Śṛingeri Maṭh (monastery) which was the seat of the Bhārati order.[11] His biographers do not mention this fact. Murāri and Kavikarṇapūra write that Chaitanya went to the south on pilgrimage as far as Rāmeśvaram and returned after worshipping Rāmeśvara Śiva (see footnote 47).

---

[6]Viśvāmbhar took initiation from Keśava Bhārati, because he was known to him and happened to be near at hand, when Viśvāmbhar decided to take *sannyāsa*. Viśvambhar's brother Viśvarūpa also became a monk. The tradition is that he took the name Śaṅkara and joined the Śaṅkarite order of Araṇya.

[7]*Murāri*, III.2.7.

[8]Vṛindāvan Dās explains the new name as 'One who awakens the consciousness of Kṛishṇa in the hearts of all'. (*Ch. Bhāgavat*, II.28.175).

[9]The monastic name 'Chaitanya' indicated that the new monk was a novice (*Brahmachāri*) of the Bhārati order. But he did not become a full-fledged monk, as he did not recite *Aham Brahmāsmi*, the *mahā-vākya* ('essence of truth') of the Bhārati order.

Chaitanya's close companion, Purushottama Achārya took the name Dāmodar after his initiation as monk. He was a 'Svarupa' or novice of the Tīrtha order.

[10]In the *Chaitanya Chandrodaya* drama (Act V, verses 21f) Advaita criticizes Chaitanya for having joined that particular *asrama* which is so much liked by people belonging to the Advaita (school). Chaitanya answers laughing 'Oh Advaita, remember that we do not belong to the advaita'.

[11]A śloka locates the Śrīngeri monastery at Rāmeśvaram (quoted in the Gauḍīya Mission edition of the *Chaitanya Charitāmṛita* p. 506)

Chaturtho dakshinānmayah Śrīgeryām vartate Maṭhaḥ.

* * *

Padani trīṇi khyātāni Sarasvatī, Bhārati, Purī
Varāha devatā yatra kshetra Rāmeśvara badyet

Two Bengali books by well-known writers *Puṅyatīrtha Bhārat* by Svāmī Divyātmānanda, p. 210, and *Nilakaṇṭha Himālaya* by Avadhut p. 123 give the following information:

kshetra—Rāmeśvaram: Presiding deity—Varāha: Brahmachāri—Chaitanya: Tīrtha—Tuṅgabhadrā. After the decline of the Śrīngeri Maṭh at Rāmesvaram, the Sṛingagiri Maṭh on the Tungabhadra in Karnataka came to be known as Śrīngeri.

(iii) Sojourn at Santipur

After entering the monastic order Chaitanya wandered aimlessly for three days. Then his associates persuaded him to accompany them to the house of Advaita at Śāntipur (twelve miles from Navadvīpa). He spent three days in the house of Advaita before he decided to go on pilgrimage to south India.

(iv) Probable Motives for Settling at Puri

Śachī met her son, who had turned hermit, at Śāntipur. According to Kṛishṇadās Kavirāj, she told Advaita and others "Let him live at Nilāchala (Puri) which is as it were, next door to Navadvīpa. People are continuously passing between the two places and I shall always get his news."[12]

Orissa was the only independent Hindu kingdom in northern India at that time. Pratāpa Rudra was known to be a religiously minded king. Orissa was associated with the memory of Śrīdhar Svāmī, who wrote the *Bhāvārtha Dīpikā* commentary of the *Bhāgavata,* in which he attempted to combine the advaita teachings of Saṅkara with the emotionalism of the Bhāgavatas.[13] Mādhavendra Puri, the preceptor of Īśvara Puri, also came

---

[12] *Ch. Ch.* II.3.182-183. Chaitanya said, "I am at Nīlāchala at the command of my mother. (*Ch. Ch.* II.2.9). But according to Murāri (*kāvya* III.4.23) and Vṛindāvan Dās (*Ch. Bhāgavat*, III 2.7) Chaitanya himself decided to settle at Puri.

We get an idea of the Jagannāth road to Puri from Jayānanda's description of Chaitanya's journey. After crossing the border of Orissa, Chaitanya proceeded via the following places Jaleśvar—Amardā-Vamsdā (near Basta)-Rāmachandrapur and Remunā (both near Balasore)—Soro—Bhadrak—Dhāmnagar—Jājpur. Jayānanda writes in his *Chaitanya Mangal* that from Jājpur, the Master went to Purushottampur (12 kilometres from Jājpur) after crossing the Mandākini. This river now called the Dudhei is almost dried. From Purushottampur he reached the north bank of the Birupā. There is even now a track from Purushottampur to Balichandrapur on the Birupā. Chaitanya followed the Birupa bank up to Chowdwar. He crossed the Mahanadi and reached Cuttack. From Cuttack he went to Bhubaneswar. A few miles after leaving Bhubaneswar, he crossed the Bhargavi and proceeded towards Puri.

During the Muslim rule in Orissa, a new alignment of the route to Cuttack was made. A road was constructed from Baruan near Purushottampur to Cuttack via Padampur on the Mahanadi. The Muslims also made a new road to Puri from Bhubaneswar via Pipli. From 1813 Captain Sackville of the East India Company began the construction of a new Jagannāth road which connected Baruan with Cuttack by a new road via Jagatpur on the Mahanadi bank.

[13] S. De, *History of the Vaishṇava Faith and Movement in Bengal*, p. 17. Chaitanya had highest esteem for Śrīdhar's commentary of the *Bhāgavata* (*Ch. Ch.* III.7.114). According to tradition, Śrīdhara lived at Mareijñā near Remuṇā in the Balasore district. A family in that village claims to be his descendants (P. Acharya—*Studies in Orissan History, Archaeology and Archives*, p. 413).

to Puri from Vṛindāvana for the *darśan* (sight) of Jagannāth and to take sandal-wood for his deity Gopāla.

It may be a fact that Chaitanya wanted to settle in Orissa, which was, if we believe Jayānanda, the country of his ancestors. Jayānanda writes in his *Chaitanya Maṅgal* (p. 96) that 'Chaitanya's ancestors lived at Jājpur. They antagonised Rājā Bhramara and fled to Sylhet out of fear'.[14] Jayānanda's statement may indicate the migration of a Brahman family from Jājpur.[15] It does not seem probable that the family fled away out of fear, even if we assume that Chaitanya's ancestor Madhukara had intimate relations with the deposed Gaṅga king. In one of his inscriptions in the Jagannāth temple, Kapilendra expresses his devotion to the Brahmans. Instead of migrating to distant Sylhet, Madhukara might have taken shelter in densely forested west Orissa, over which the Gajapati king had hardly any authority.

(v) Pilgrimage of Chaitanya

Chaitanya told Advaita about his decision to go on pilgrimage to South India before settling at Puri. Vṛindāvan Dās writes that Advaita tried to persuade him to postpone the journey, pointing out the hazardous condition that prevailed at that time. But the Master was adamant. Accompanied by four companions he began his journey to the south.[16]

---

[14]Rājā Bhramara has been identified with Kapilendra who is called 'Bhramaravara' in v. 4 of an inscription of a private person at Gopinathpur in the Cuttack district. (J.A.S.B., 1900) Bhramaravara is an honorific title. It is also used as a name. According to Jayānanda, Madhukar Miśra, a *Vaidika* Brahman, left Jājpur and migrated to Sylhet. His grandson Jagannāth Miśra was forced to leave Sylhet because of drought and lawlessness (*Chaitanya Mangal.* 'Nadiā khaṇḍa). Jagannāth Miśra settled at Navadvīpa which was a great seat of Sanskrit learning.

Chaitanya belonged to the Vatsya *gotra* (sept.) *Murāri* I.3.20). "There are still hundreds of Brahman families in Orissa belonging to the Vatsya *gotra*" (K.N. Mahapatra: *O.H.R.J.* Vol. II, p. 46). It is said that Chaitanya's ancestors lived at Dasarajpur, a village near Chhatiā in the Jājpur subdivision of the Cuttack district.

[15]Jājpur was a town of the Brahmans (*Brahman-nagara, Murāri* III.6.15: *Ch. Bhāgavat* III.2). According to tradition Chaitanya's ancestors were western *Vaidika* Brahmans. "If the tradition that the Ganga kings brought the Jājpur Brahmans from Kanauj is true, then the Jājpur Brahmans are to be considered as western *Vaidika*", N.N. Vasu: *Visvakosh*, p. 487 (1909).

Similarly, some Brahmans from north Bengal migrated to Orissa. Raṇaka Raṇa Bhañja made land grants to some persons who had come from Puṇḍravardhana of Vareṇḍri Maṇḍala. One such donee belonged to the Vatsya *gotra* (Dr. K.C. Panigrahi: *O.H.R.J.* Vol. XI, p. 156). Another donee from Vareṇḍri Maṇḍala was Bhaṭṭa Damuni Ghosha who belonged to the *Arishtasena gotra* (S.N. Rajguru: *The Inscriptions of Orissa*, Vol. VI (in Press).

[16]Chaitanya was accompanied by Nityānanda, Jagadānanda, Dāmodar, and Mukunda (*Ch. Chandrodaya drama*, VI. 5) Nityānanda had knowledge about the route,

(vi) Journey to Puri

Chhatrabhog: The main stream of the Ganga flowed at that time through the Hooghly and the Ādigaṅga. Chaitanya followed the route by the side of the Ganga and reached Chhatrabhog, situated about 25 miles south-west of Calcutta in the Mathurāpur Police station of the 24 Parganas district. Chhatrabhog was famous for the submerged Śiva image named Ambu Liṅga. Chaitanya worshipped the deity. Then he crossed the river by boat and reached 'Prayāga ghat' of 'Utkal Deśa'.[17] Chaitanya now proceeded towards the Suvarnarekha river. On the way, he danced in emotion and constantly chanted Kṛishṇa's name.

Jaleswar: Chaitanya reached Jaleswar on the Suvarnarekha. He bathed in the river and visited the temple of Jaleśvar Śiva. Vṛindāvan Dās writes the priests were worshipping the deity at that time. Incense and lighted lamps created a holy atmosphere. There were singers, accompanied by the musicians. The temple of Jaleśvara does not exist now. It was probably destroyed by Husain Shāh, the Sultan of Bengal.

Remuna: Remuna was the headquarters of a 'Daṇḍapāta' or district at that time. Remuna is famous for the temple of Gopīnāth. Chaitanya sang in an ecstatic mood before the image of Gopīnāth. Kavikarṇapūra in his *kāvya* (XI.78) and drama (VI.9) has mentioned a miracle. He writes that when the Master beheld Gopīnātha, his voice was choked with emotion and tears trickled down her cheeks. As he bowed down at the feet of the image, a bunch of flowers on the crown of the deity, dropped upon his head. The attendants of the deity marvelled at the sight.

It is stated in the *Chaitanya Charitāmṛita* that the Master, while worshipping Gopīnātha, recited a verse which was composed by

---

having previously visited Puri (*Ch. Bhāgavat*, I.6). There was much justification for Advaita's apprehensions. Husain Shāh, Sultan of Bengal, wanted to push back the Oriyas from the banks of the Hooghly for the safety of Satgaon. Periodical border clashes had begun from 1500, with little territorial advantages on either side. It is stated in the Idupulupaḍu grant of Pratāpa Rudra dated in November 1500 (*Archaeological Report* No. 802 of 1922) that Vīra Rudra completely defeated the king of Gauḍ. Similarly, Husain Shāh called himself 'the conqueror of Jajnagar' in his coins dated 1504-5. Taking advantage of Pratāpa Rudra's expedition to the south, Husain Shāh increased his military activities against his neighbour. Sporadic clashes had already begun when Chaitanya decided to start for Puri on his way to South India (*Ch. Chandrodaya* drama, VI.4).

[17] *Ch. Bhāgavat*. III.2 'Prayāg ghat appears to be a ghat of the Mantresvar river near Diamond Harbour'' B.B. Majumdar; C.C.U., p. 244.

Mādhavendra Puri.[18] Vṛindāvan Dās does not mention any such recitation of a verse by the Master. Kṛishṇadās Kavirāj has probably introduced the recitation to depict the *Rādhābhāva* of Chaitanya on seeing the image of Gopīnātha.[19]

The orthodox writers took Chaitanya directly from Remuna to Jajpur. But Jayānanda writes that he visited Siddheśvara Śiva at Soro on his way to Bhadrak, before he reached Jajpur.

Jajpur: Chaitanya bathed at the Daśāsvamedha ghat on the Vaitaraṇi. He went to the temple of Ādi Varāha and bowed to Holy Boar. He also visited the Virajā temple and other shrines at Jajpur. Vṛindāvan Dās writes that at Jajpur he left his followers and went somewhere. His followers had to wait for him. According to Jayānanda, he stayed in the house of his relation Kamalalochana Miśra.

Cuttack: Chaitanya reached Cuttack after crossing the river Mahanadi. His joy knew no bounds when he beheld the image of Gopāla.[20] But the presence of an ascetic with four companions did not attract public notice at the capital.

Bhubaneswar: From Cuttack, Chaitanya journeyed to Bhubaneswar. He bathed in the Vindu Sarovara tank and proceeded to the Liṅgarāja temple.

---

[18]*Ch. Ch.* II.4. 130-5.

In this poem (quoted in Rūpa Gosvāmī's *Padyāvali* No. 330) Rādhā addresses Kṛishṇa who is at Mathurā.

[19]In Orissa and in the Telugu country, the two handed images of Kṛishṇa were called both Gopīnātha and Gopāla. Murāri in his *kāvya* refers to the image of Gopāla at Remuna (III.6.3). In his grant to Poteśvara Bhaṭṭa (of Garhpadā near Balasore) Purushottama Gajapati sought the benediction of Madana Gopāla. This deity is a variation of Veṇu Gopāla, which is a flute playing Kṛishṇa image standing on its left leg (Gopinath Rao: *Hindu Iconography* Vol. I, p. 208) Kavikarṇapūra (*kāvya* II.79) and Jayānanda (*Chaitanya Mangal* p. 97) write that Chaitanya on his way to Puri visited the temple of Sākshi Gopīnātha at Cuttack. The deity Sākshi Gopāla is locally called Sākshi Gopīnātha also.

In the Telugu country, Gopīnātha was also known as Gopāla. The following temples of Veṇu Gopāla Svāmīn in the Guntur district were also called the temples of Gopīnātha (No. 572 of 1909 at Durgi: Nos. 26 & 57 of 1930 at Pulipadu and Pudu-guralla: No. 316 of 1936 at Oleru (*Archaeological Reports of the Madras Presidency*).

[20]This image was kept in a shrine within the fort of Bārabati at Cuttack. It was removed to Satyabadi in the Puri district after the Muslim conquest of Orissa. It is stated in the *Chaitanya Chandrodaya* VI. 16 that king Purushottama brought the image of Gopāla from Mahendra Deśa. The image holds '*reṇu*' (flute) by its two hands.

Śrinādha Bhaṭṭa, the court-poet of Allāda Reḍḍi, writes in his *Kāśi Khaṇḍam* (V. 9) that the image of Madana Gopāla has manifested itself in the city of Rajamahendra-varam.

Vṛindāvan Dās writes that out of ecstasy, he danced before the Śiva Liṅga. According to Murāri, he recited a hymn in honour of Śiva. The first two lines of hymn are translated here. "Oh Lord of the universe. O Lord of the Spirits. O Śiva. I always pay thee my obeisance. Thou hast taken young Moon, who has arisen from the current of the Gaṅgā, as thy head-dress. Thou hast given joy to the eyes of Gaurī."

It is stated that he also visited another Śiva temple in a lonely place, probably the temple of Brahmeśvara. It is surprising that Chaitanya's biographers have not specifically mentioned his visit to the Vishṇu temple of Ananta Vāsudeva, situated on the Vindu Sarovara, which he must have visited after bathing in the tank.

Kamalpur: After spending the night at Bhubaneswar, Chaitanya and his companions continued their journey. Chaitanya crossed the Bhargavi near Bālakāṭhi, a few miles away from Bhubaneswar, and proceeded towards Puri. He reached Kamalpur on the west bank of the Bhargavi. He halted there to visit the Kapoteśvara temple.[21] Before he went to the Kapoteśvara temple, Chaitanya left his monastic staff (*daṇḍa*) with Nityānanda, who, out of impulse, broke the staff and threw the pieces into the river.[22]

Kṛishṇadās Kavirāj writes that Chaitanya witnessed the spire of the Jagannāth temple from the vicinity of the Kapoteśvara temple and was overcome with emotion. On reaching Atharanallā* he came to his senses and asked Nityānanda for his staff. When he heard about its fate, "he was angry and went alone to see Jagannāth".[23] Probably as a punishment, he forbade his companions to accompany him.

(vii) At the Jagannāth temple

The Master ran and entered into the temple. His frenzy knew no bounds when he saw the image of Jagannāth. He rushed to embrace the image

[21]The Kapoteśvara temple is situated near the Janakdeipur railway station. There are three mouths of the Bhargavi river near the temple. One of the streams, called 'Daṇḍa Bhaṅgā' (breaking of the staff) flows towards the Atharanalla bridge. There is now no village named Kamalpur. It was not far off from Chandanpur on the east bank of the Bhargavi. The spire of the Jagannāth temple is not visible from the Kapoteśvara temple. It can be seen only from a spot called 'Tulasi Chaurā', about seven miles from Puri.

[22]*Ch. Ch.* II.5, 151. Kṛishṇadās Kavirāj's statement (*Ch. Ch.* II.5) is supported by Murāri (*kāvya* III.1.15) and Kavikarṇapūra (*kāvya* (XI.81) But Vṛindāvan Dās writes that Nityānanda broke the staff at Jaleswar (III.2) to make it a trivial incident.

*Atharanallā is an old bridge consisting of 18 small arches over a small stream. The town of Puri begins from other side of the stream.

[23]*Ch. Ch.* II.1.98 : *Kāvya* of Kavikarṇapūra: XI.81.

and was forcibly prevented by the Pratihāris (door-keepers). Stricken down by the force of his emotion, he fell down senseless on the floor. The Pratihāris thought him to be a mentally demented monk and were going to throw him out. But luckily, Vāsudeva Sārvabhauma, a great vedantic scholar, was present in the temple at that time. With the help of the attendants, Śārvabhauma carried the unconscious monk to his house.

By that time, Nityānanda, Mukunda and other followers reached the main gate of the temple. They anxiously enquired about a monk who had shortly come before them. They met Gopināth, the brother-in-law of Śārvabhauma. Gopināth was acquainted with Mukunda at Navadvīpa. He gave the information that a Śannyāsī had fainted inside the Jagannāth temple and he had been taken to the house of Vāsudeva Sārvabhauma.[21]

(viii) Vāsudeva Sārvabhauma

Vāsudeva Sārvabhauma was an erudite scholar in Vedānta. He migrated to Orissa along with his family and settled in the holy city of Puri. Sārvabhauma was widely respected for his piety and scholarship. He was well acquainted with king Pratāpa Rudra. He daily visited the Jagannāth temple and he saved Chaitanya from being manhandled by the servitors of the Jagannāth temple. The Master, after regaining consciousness, thanked Sārvabhauma for bringing him to his house. Sārvabhauma found out that his father knew Chaitanya's maternal grandfather well.

The venerable scholar was sorry that a young man of twenty-four years only, had taken monastic vow, and that of the Bhārati order which

---

[24]Krishṇadās Kavirāj has substantially followed the narration of Vṛindāvan Dās. In their *kāvyas*, Murāri (III.10.17 & III.11.4-16) and Kavikarṇapūra (XI 85-86 & XII.1) made conflicting statements regarding Chaitanya's first visit to the Jagannāth temple. In the *Chaitanya Chandrodaya* drama (VI. 29) it is stated that the companions of Chaitanya apprehended that it might not be possible for them to enter the Jagannāth temple without the help of the royal officers (*Rāja Furusha*) as they were foreigners (*para deśi*). But Sārvabhauma and his son Chandaneśvara who, according to the drama, took Chaitanya and his companions to the Jagannāth temple were not royal officers. It is not possible to believe that Chaitanya, who raced from Śāntipur to behold Jagannāth, went to the house of Sārvabhauma and took rest.

Kavikarṇapur does not make any reference to the fainting of Chaitanya in the Jagannāth temple in his *kāvya* and drama. By the time he wrote the drama, the tradition that Chaitanya passed away into the image of Jagannāth was taking root in Orissa. It was believed that the Master twice tried to embrace the image of Jagannāth and on the second occasion he merged himself into the image. This accounts for the reticence of Kavikarṇapūra, while describing Chaitanya's emotional fervour at the sight of Jagannāth for the first time. Kavikarṇapūra, like other Gaūḍiya Vaishṇavas, was opposed to the conception of Chaitanya's merger into Jagannāth.

did not rank high among the ten orders of the Śaṅkara school. He wanted to teach Vedānta to Chaitanya for a better spiritual outlook. He invited Chaitanya to stay for some days in his house. A learned disputation took place for seven days. Kavikarṇapūra has described the disputation between Sārvabhauma and Chaitanya in his *kāvya* (XII) and drama (VI). It began with Sārvabhauma's exposition of monistic doctrines of Vedānta. Chaitanya showed fallacy in his arguments by expounding dualistic Vaishṇava tenets and by giving new interpretations of the ślokas quoted by Sārvabhauma.

Sārvabhauma was probably more attracted by the personality of the Master and the sincerity of his exposition of the Bhakti doctrine than by his erudition. He now became a disciple of Chaitanya which was the "first major achievement" of the Chaitanya movement in Orissa (S.K. De). Thus, the young ascetic who could change the life-long convictions of a veteran philosopher, became an important person. Kavikarṇapūra writes in his drama (canto VI) that when the Master went to the Jagannāth temple, he was well-received by the servitors of the temple.

(ix) Sojourn at Puri

Chaitanya started from Sāntipur in the second week of Phalguna. Kṛishṇadās Kavirāj writes that he reached Puri in time to see the Dola Yātrā* which took place on the 29th Phalguna—23 February 1510.[25] At that time, it would be difficult to reach Puri from Sāntipur in 16 or 17 days. Moreover Chaitanya halted at different places to visit the temples. Kānāi Khunṭiā writes that the young ascetic reached Puri during the 'Benṭa Yātrā'.[26] According to Kavikarṇapūra, Chaitanya stayed at Puri for eighteen days.[27]

He wanted to go to the south to visit the holy places. Chaitanya started without further rest to cover a long distance before the setting of the rains. He was persuaded to take a companion with him as attendant, to carry his extra cloth and the water pot, as his hands were almost always engaged in prayer.[28]

---

*The Dola Yātrā or the swinging festival is associated with the worship of Kṛishṇa.

[25]*Ch. Ch.* II.7.4.

[26]*Mahābhāva Prakāśa* canto 3. 'Benṭa Yātrā' is an annual festivity, held in the month of Chaitra. The kings of Orissa used to go for hunting on that day.

[27]*Kavikarṇapūra's kāvya* XII.94. Kṛishṇadas Kavirāj writes that the Master started from Puri in the month of Vaisakha.

[28]*Ch. Ch.* II.7.36. It may be a fact that his companions were physically exhausted by the strain of the journey from Śāntipur to Puri and none of them could accompany him. The biographers of Chaitanya are all silent regarding the hardship of the journey to Puri. Kṛishṇadās even writes that the pilgrims from Bengal came regularly for

(x) Political condition in 1510

Pratāpa Rudra was not present in Orissa at that time, having gone to the south to war against Vijayanagar.[29] According to the Telugu work, the *Rāyavachakamu,* the Sultans of the Deccan informed the Gajapati king Kṛishṇadeva Raya the king of Vijayanagar, was making preparations to attack Orissa. He was cautioned to be alert and to garrison his fortresses.[30] Pratāpa Rudra proceeded to the South for defensive measures.[31]

Husain Shah seized this opportunity. The *Mādalā Pañji* (Jagannāth temple Chronicle) states that '*Amura Surathāna*' (Amir Sultan) '*Patiśā*' (Padshah) of Gaur entered Puri and destroyed some images in the Jagannāth temple. It is further stated that the Gajapati king, on receipt of the news, hurried towards the capital and chased the enemy away. The Sultan took shelter in the fort of Mandāran (Hooghly district, West Bengal) which was closely besieged. Govinda Vidyādhar, an officer of the king, now became a traitor. Pratāpa Rudra was compelled to make peace with the enemy.[32]

(xi) Date of the Muslim invasion

When did Husain Shah invade Orissa? He did not invade before April 1510. The splendour of the Śiva temple at Jaleswar near the border has been described by Vṛindāvan Dās. Chaitanya visited the temple on his

twenty years to see the chariot festivals and to meet the Master (*Ch. Ch.* II.1.45).

Even after the construction of partly metalled road in the second decade of the 19th century, the pilgrims suffered greatly. They trudged their way for some hundreds of miles across large rivers through dense forests infested by robbers. Food and shelter were not always available. At last, worn out by the fatigue of the journey, the pilgrims used to reach Puri 'with feet bound in rags, plastered with dirt and blood'. Conditions were certainly worse in the 16th century. Kavikarṇapūra refers to the fear of bandits (*Dasyu bhaya*) on the road in his drama (VIII).

[29]*Chaitanya Bhāgavat*, III.3.269.

[30]Dr. N. Venkataramanayya: *The Sources of Vijayanagar History*, p. 130.

[31]We learn from the Guṇḍlapalem plates (*Archaeological Report* No 185 of 1933-34) that the Gajapati made a grant in the Nellore district in January 1510.

[32]Prachi edition of the *Mādalā Pañji*, p. 52.

It is stated in *Mahābhāva Prakasa* by Kānāi Khuntia that 'Surasthān Ghāzi Isimili' (Ismail Ghazi was the general of the Sultan) advanced as far as Nilāchala, during the absence of the king in the south. The priests secretly removed the image of Jagannāth from the temple and took it to the Chilka coast. Pratāpa Rudra hurriedly came back and chased the enemy up to Mandāran. But he could not take the fort. There is no reference to Govinda Vidyādhara in this book.

Husain Shah's destruction of a large number of temples in Orissa has also been mentioned by Vṛindāvan Dās (*Ch. Bhāgavat*, III.4.67 & 78).

way to Puri. Thus the Muslim invasion took place after 1510. Pratāpa Rudra was present in the Nellore district in October 1510 and made a grant.[33] It records that the king of Gauḍa fled on the approach of the Gajapati king. It may be cited as an evidence of Husain Shah's invasion and retreat from Orissa between May and June 1510. Assuming that he invaded Orissa in May or June 1510, it was not possible for Pratāpa Rudra to march northward as far as Mandāran in Bengal and to come back to the Nellore district before the rainy season when bad roads and unbridged rivers swollen with flood waters forbade military operations in Orissa.

It is more probable that Husain Shah invaded Orissa after the rainy season in 1511. Pratāpa Rudra hurried northward. Taking advantage of his absence, Timmarasu, the minister of Kṛishṇadeva Raya advanced with an army and occupied a portion of the province of Koṇḍaviḍu, then a part of Orissa.[34] Timmarasu withdrew on Pratāpa Rudra's return to the South. In January 1512, Pratāpa Rudra made gifts in the Nellore district.[35] The sequence of events will be clear from the following time table:

October 1511	—Husain Shah invades Orissa
November 1511	—Pratāpa Rudra chases him up to Mandāran. A contingent under Timmarasu occupies a part of the province of Koṇḍaviḍu
December 1511	—Pratāpa Rudra hurries back to his southern frontier. Timmarasu withdraws
January 1512	—Pratāpa Rudra made gifts in the Nellore district

(xii) Journey to Rajamahendri

Chaitanya started with only one companion. He wended his way along the Chilka coast and halted at Āḷālnāth, about 13 miles from Puri.* From Āḷāḷnāth, he went to Srikurmam (8 miles south of Chicacole) and worshipped the image of Kūrma. Then he reached Simhachalam and made obeisance to the deity Nṛisimha. The Master rapturously sang in praise of the deity. He continued his journey and reached Vidyanagar.[36] He halted on the bank of the Godavari.

---

[33]The Velicherla grant dated 4 October 1510: A.R. No. 12 of 1920-21.

[34]Inscription at Gonugunta dated 1 November 1511: *Nellore District Inscriptions*, Vol. II, p. 789.

[35]The Guḍimelapadu plates: A.R. No. 56 of 1945-46.

*There is reference to Allālanātha in a thirteenth century inscription (*Epigraphia Indica*, Vol. XXXI, p. 95).

[36]Kṛishṇadās probably meant Rajamahendri in his reference to Vidyānagar. The sacred hill of Vidiādri at Rajamahendri was praised by Śrinādha Bhaṭṭa in his poem, *Kāsi Khaṇḍdam* (v. 9). Rājamahendri was one of the three southern provinces of the kingdom of Orissa.

Kṛishṇadās Kavirāj gives a lengthy description of Chaitanya's meeting with Rāmānanda. He writes that Rāy Rāmānanda, Governor of the province of Rājamahendri came to take bath in the Godavari, accompanied by Brahmans and musicians. When Rāmānanda got down from the litter, he saw an ascetic standing at some distance. He wondered as he gazed at the radiant face of the ascetic. Rāmānanda prostrated himself at the Master's feet in ecstasy. The latter said: "Rise and chant Kṛishṇa's name." When Rāmānanda got up, Chaitanya asked him: "Are you Rāy Rāmānanda?" He answered: "Yes, I am that slave: a vile Śudra.*" Passionately did the Master embrace him. Both fell down on the ground, deeply overpowered by loving emotion. Perspiring, weeping, with their hairs standing on the end, they lisped 'Kṛishṇa' Kṛishṇa'. The Brahmans were surprised at this sight. They said: "Why does the Sannyāsi weep after embracing a Śudra?" Chaitanya and Rāmānanda held scholastic discourses for some days, which were described by Kṛishṇadas Kavirāj "with theological relish and precision."

At Puri, Sārvabhauma had advised Chaitanya to meet Rāmānanda. 'Do not ignore him because he is a Śudra and a householder' said Sārvabhauma. 'He is an erudite scholar and is the best exponent of the *Bhakti* faith.'[37]

Before the advent of Chaitanya in Orissa, a few Oriya Vaishṇavas were inspired by the devotional faith of Mādhavendra Puri and by the poems of Vidyāpati. Rāmānanda probably came in contact with Rāghava Puri, a disciple of Mādhavendra Puri.[38] Love songs on Rādhā and Kṛishṇa were written in the Maithili dialect by Vidyāpati, who "flourished between AD 1390 and 1490."[39]

The pilgrims who came to Puri from Mithilā in north Bihar spread those songs in Orissa. The sensuous lyrics of Jayadeva also gave inspiration for the composition of erotic poems on Rādhā-Krishna. Purushottama Gajapati, father of Pratāpa Rudra, supplicated blessings from the union of Rādhā and Kṛishṇa in the prologue of his drama entitled *Abhinava Veṇī Samharanam.* Rāmānanda in his Jagannāth Vallabha drama, drew inspiration from Jayadeva's *Gīta Govinda* while describing the amorous love scenes of Rādhā and Kṛishṇa.

Rāmānanda was the first great exponent of the creed of the new

---

*At that time, the word 'Śudra' denoted all caste Hindus who were not Brahmans or Kshatriyas.

[37]*Ch. Ch.* II. 7.61-62.

[38]About Rāghava little is known. There is a legend that Rāghava was an Oriya Brahman. Kavikarṇapūra refers to him as a person of saintly character. (*Gauragaṇoddeṣa Dipikā*, ślokas 96-7).

[39]Dr. M. Sahidullah: 'The date of Vidyapati': *Indian Historical Quarterly*, Vol. XX, p. 217.

faith. Kṛishṇadās Kavirāj described, not what Rāmānanda had actually said, but what he should have said, during his religious discourses with Chaitanya at Rājamahendri. So we are to depend on Kavikarṇapūra who had better knowledge of the incident.

Kṛishṇadās cites from the *kāvya* of Kavikarṇapūra, Rāmānanda's exposition of the graded means of devotion to Kṛishṇa. Rāmānanda dealt with 'the basic theory of *rasa* (primary emotions) which was later developed by the Gauḍīya Vaishṇavas.'[40] Kṛishṇadās quotes a dialogue in question-answer form from the *Chaitanya Chandrodaya* drama (vii. 8-10). During this dialogue with Chaitanya, Rāmānanda explained that the most valuable possession for a devotee is love for Kṛishṇa and that the love songs on Rādhā and Kṛishṇa are sweetest. Lastly, he pointed out that Vṛindāvana is the seat of the eternal dalliance of Rādhā and Kṛishṇa. Kṛishṇadās Kavirāj has quoted a poem in the Maithili dialect, composed by Ray Rāmānanda, from the *kāvya* of Kavikarṇapūra (See chapter VIII). The poem referes to king Pratāpa Rudra in the colophon. But Kṛishṇadās omits that reference which he considered unbecoming for a devotee like Rāmānanda.

Chaitanya asked Rāmānanda to give up his post and to go to Puri. 'We shall pass our days joyously talking about Kṛishṇa' he said. After his return to Puri from the south, the Master told Sārvabhauma about his contact with different sects of the Vaishṇavas, and also with the Śaivas and the *Pāshandis* (Buddhists) 'But Bhattāchārya' he said 'I like Rāmānanda's doctrine.'[41]

(xiii) Journey beyond Rajamahendri

From Rajamahendri, Chaitanya proceeded to Srirangam on the Kaveri. Then he reached Rameśvaram and worshipped Rāmesvara Śiva. He also saw Setubandha.[42] So long Kṛishṇadās Kavirāj takes help of Murāri and Kavikarṇapūra in his description of Chaitanya's journey to Rāmeśvaram. Now he takes help of his own imagination to describe Chaitanya's itinerary in Karnataka and Maharashtra. He writes that the Master took bath in the sacred site known as Dhanutīrtha when he went to Setubandha.[43] Kṛishṇadās takes Chaitanya from Dhanutīrtha near Rāmeśvaram to another Dhanutīrtha in Gujarat. He wanted to refute the idea that the Master went only as far as Rāmeśvaram and returned after worshipping

---

[40] A.K. Majumdar. *Chaitanya: His life and doctrine*, p. 181.

[41] '*Kimtu Bhattāchārya, Rāmānanda matam eva me ruchitam*' *Chaitanya Chandrodaya* VI, p. 255 (Chowkhamba series).

[42] *Murāri*, III.16.5–6: Kavikarṇapūra's kavya XIII.32-33.

[43] *Ch. Ch.* II. 9.199. It is said that Rāmachandra's *dhanu* (bow) partly broke the Setubandha (bridge joining Bhārata with Lankā) as desired by Bibhisaṇa.

the image of Rāmeśvara Śiva. He satisfied the sentiments of the pious Vaishṇavas by making Chaitanya visit the famous Vaīshṇava temple of Adi Kesava in Malabar. We are told that from Karnāṭaka, the Master went to the north as far as Gujarat. But he did not visit Dvārakā which is associated with the memory of Kṛishṇa. He saw Dhanutīrtha,[44] bathed in the river Nirbindha near Ujjain, and began his return journey. Chaitanya came to Kuśavarta, the source of the Godavari, near Nasik in Maharashtra. Then instead of going straight to Puri, Chaitanya again returned to Rajamahendri, across the Deccan, to meet Rāmānanda.

Kṛishṇadās Kavirāj gives a new information, not mentioned by Murāri and Kavikarṇapūra. He wants to show that Rāmānanda's conclusions are supported by two earlier texts on Kṛishṇa *bhakti*. Kṛishṇadās Kavirāj writes that the Master found a copy of the *Brahma Samhita* from a temple on the river Payasvini and a copy of the *Krishṇa Karṇāmrita* at a place on the bank of the Kṛishṇavenna river in Maharashtra.[45]

In his description of the itinerary of Chaitanya in South India Kṛishṇdās Kavirāj shows his ignorance about the locations of many places mentioned by him.[46] According to him Chaitanya goes to the Gajendra mokshaṇa *tīrtha* in the Trivandrum district and then goes back to the Tirunelaveli district to visit Pānāgarh. Later, he leaves for Champtāpur in the Trivandrum district to worship the images of Rāma and Lakshmaṇa. Then we find him at Kanyākumari in the Tirunelaveli district. We may

[44]Probably Kṛishṇadās meant Manutīrtha near the Narmada. There is reference to Manutīrtha in the *Bhāgavata*. Nityānanda during his pilgrimage in northern India visited Manutīrtha. It is difficult to explain why Kṛishṇadas Kavirāj took Chaitanya as far as Dhanutīrtha (*Ch. Ch.* II.9.311). Many pilgrims travelled from Rāmeśvaram to Dvārakā, where Śaṅkara founded the Śāradā Maṭh. From them Kṛishṇadās got some idea about the places on the route. But there was no such pilgrim route from Nāsik near the source of the Godavari to Rajamahendri on the mouth of the Godavari. Consequently, Kṛishṇadās Kavirāj made no references to the places where Chaitanya halted before he reached Rajamahendri, as he had no idea.

[45]The authorship of the *Karṇāmrita* has been ascribed to Līlāsuka Vilvamaṅgala. It appears that Chaitanya was made to visit Maharashtra in order to obtain a manuscript of the *Kṛishṇa Karṇāmrita*. Kṛishṇadās Kavirāj wrote a commentary of the *Kṛishṇa Karṇāmrita* entitled *Saranga Rangadā* which was based on the commentary of that work by Gopāla Bhaṭṭa.

A. Sen points out that at that time in South India, the Sanskrit manuscripts were written in regional characters. In his opinion, Chaitanya found a copy of the *Brahma Saṃhitā* written in Malayalam characters and a copy of the *Krishna Karṇāmrita* written in Marathi characters and got them copied.

(A. Sen: *Itihaser Sri Chaitanya*, p. 118)

[46]It appears from the close similarity of the description of Kṛishṇadās Kavirāj with the itinerary of Baladeva in the *Bhāgavata* that some of the place names in the Charitāmṛita have been taken from the Bhāgavata.

cite another instance of confusion. Chaitanya proceeds to Uḍipi on the Tungabhadra in Karnataka. Then he goes to Phalgutirtha in the Anantapur district. Next he visits Triṭakupa near Cochin.

(xiv) Return journey

According to the contemporary biographers, Chaitanya went up to Rāmeśvaram and returned to Rajamahendri by the same route.[47] But Kṛishṇadās Kavirāj takes him to western India. Chaitanya again came to Rajamahendri to hand over the manuscripts of the *Brahma Saṃhitā* and the *Kṛishṇa Karṇāmṛita* to Rāmānanda, who would have gone to Puri after a few months. Rāmānanda had the manuscripts copied. Rāmānanda could not accompany the Master to Puri, as he was not yet relieved from his post at Rajamahendri. On his way to Puri Chaitanya halted at Ālālanāth. He reached Puri in 1512 before the Snāna Yātrā.*

(xv) Pratāpa Rudra's homage to the Master

The Gajapati king was a devout Vaishṇava. His curiosity about Chaitanya was aroused when he received the letter of Rāmānanda, expressing his desire to resign and to live in the company of the Master. Till then, he had not heard about this young ascetic who had come from Navadvīpa, visiting south India on pilgrimage.

This accounts for the fact that the king did not try to meet Chaitanya when he passed through the Nellore district on his way to Srirangam. The Gudimelapaḍu plates dated January 1512, refer to Pratāpa Rudra's gifts in the Nellore district. He went back to his capital in February or March 1512. At Cuttack, he heard about the 'conversion' of Sārvabhauma and sent for him. The king told Sārvabhauma that he wanted to meet Chaitanya. Sārvabhauma informed Rāmānanda about the king's desire. When Chaitanya came back to Puri and settled there, Rāmānanda pleaded for the king. But according to the *Chaitanya Chandrodaya* drama, VII, the Master categorically refused to meet a king.

Sārvabhauma advised the king to meet Chaitanya during the *Ratha Yātrā*,** when he would get tired and take rest after dancing and singing

---

[47]Kavikarṇapūra: *Kāvya* (XIII-32-34): drama (VII.23) *Setubandha tataḥ pratyagamana: Murāri*, III. 16.8. It is stated in the kāvyas of Murāri and Kavikarṇapūra that on his way back Chaitanya visited the temple of Ranganātha or Raṅgadeva at Śrīrangam (2 miles north of Trichinopoly).

*Snāna Yātrā or the festival of sacred bath in the temple of Jagannāth is held in the month of Jyestha (May-June). After the festival the deities are kept away from public view for fifteen days.

**The Chariot or Car festival is held on the second day of full moon in the month

before the chariot of Jagannāth. Kṛishṇadās Kavirāj writes that during the chariot festival, the Master danced in emotion and fell down exhausted. Pratāpa Rudra picked him up. Chaitanya regained his senses and was sorry for being touched by a person 'steeped in the worldly affairs.'[48]

After the festival, the Master lay on the ground in a grove and his eyes were closed. The king met the Master, dressed in the garb of a Vaishṇava. He touched Chaitanya's feet, while reciting from the *Bhāgavata* X.31. The Master's joy knew no bounds and he embraced the king.[49] As requested by Sārvabhauma, the king arranged the house of Kāśi Miśra, the temple Superintendent, as the residence of the Master.

(xvi) Chaitanya at Puri in 1512-14

It was greatly talked about that a great saint had come to Puri and pious Vaishṇavas flocked there to pay homage to the Master. After his return from pilgrimage to the south, Chaitanya stayed for some days in the house of Sārvabhauma, before he shifted to the house of Kāśi Miśra.[50]

Svarūp Dāmodar, a Brahman from Navadvīpa, became a monk and came to Puri from Vārānasi. The Master witnessed the chariot festival for the first time in 1512 and his ecstatic joy at the sight of Jagannāth has been vividly described by Kṛishṇadās Kavirāj in the *Chaitanya Charitāmṛita.* He sported in the Indradumnya tank at Puri, forcing the aged Advaita to join him.[51] During the Janmāshṭami festival, he dressed like a *Gopa* (milkman) and played with a stick.[52] All the prominent Gauḍiya Vaishṇavas, Advaita, Gadādhar Paṇḍit, Śrīvās and Vakreśvar had come

---

of Āsharha (June-July). Jagannāth with his brother Balarāma and sister Subhadrā leave the temple that day. They are placed on chariots and taken to another temple called the Guṇḍichā house in a mile long procession. They stay there for a week and then return to the main temple.

[48]*Ch. Ch.* II. 13.172. Kavikarṇapūra does not mention this incident in his *kāvya* or drama. Kṛishṇadās Kavirāj adds that Chaitanya agreed to meet the son of Pratāpa Rudra. When he came, Chaitanya embraced him. The prince, referred to in the *Charitāmrita*, may be either Kakhāruadeva or Kāluādeva, the two worthless sons of Pratāpa Rudra.

[49]*Chaitanya Chandrodaya* drama VIII. 54.

[50]As there was constantly a huge crowd in the house of Sārvabhauma (*Ch. Chandrodaya* VIII) the Master preferred Kāśi Miśra's house; 'the place being lonely' (*Ch. Ch.* II. 10.21)

Kāśi Miśra's house is now called the Rādhākānta Math. Chaitanya lived in a 'Gambhiri' which in Oriya means a small side room with one entrance. The cell in which he lived has only a small aperture for ventilation.

[51]Kavikarṇapūra's kāvya XVIII. 14.

[52]Kavikarṇapūra's kāvya XVIII. 50. During the Janmāshtami festival to celebrate the birth of Kṛishṇa, it is customary to act as a milkman.

to Puri to see the Master and to participate in the chariot festival. Gadādhar Paṇḍit and Svarūp Dāmodar permanently stayed at Puri. Gadādhar Paṇḍit took charge of the Gopīnāth temple, while Svarūp Dāmodar became an indispensable companion of the Master. Out of the four companions, who had accompanied Chaitanya to Puri from Bengal, Nityānanda and Mukunda Datta went back to Bengal, while Jagadānanda Paṇḍit and Dāmodar remained at Puri for some years.

The Gauḍiya Vaishṇavas could not resist the desire to see the Master again. So in spite of the hardship of the journey, many of them again came to Puri during the chariot festival in 1513.

(xvii) Journey to Bengal

Chaitanya wanted to go to Bengal and to proceed towards Vṛindāvana from Bengal. But he was persuaded by Rāmānanda and Sārvabhauma to postpone the journey. He started in 1514 in the fifth year of his sannyāsa.[53] He passed via Bhubaneswar. At Cuttack he halted in a garden house. King Pratāpa Rudra hastened to meet the Master. Chaitanya embraced him. The king ordered all officers in his kingdom to arrange accommodation for the Master and his followers during the journey.

In the evening, Chaitanya bathed in the ghat of the Mahanadi at Tulsipur. The queens of Pratāpa Rudra[54] were mounted on covered litters on the backs of elephants, which were drawn up in a line along the route. As the Master did not meet women, they made obeisance from a distance. In moonlit night, Chaitanya crossed the river Mahanadi and halted at Chowdwar. He was accompanied by two officers, Harichandan and Mangrāj and also by Rāmānanda. Some Gauḍiya disciples also went with him. At Bhadrak, Chaitanya bade farewell to Rāmānanda after a touching scene.[55]

He wended his way to the frontier of Orissa. There he was told that the territories of the Yāvana king extends up to Pichhaldā. None dares to cross the river Mantresvar.[56] Chaitanya was advised not to cross

---

[53]*Ch. Ch.* II.16.86. He left Puri on the Vijaya Daśamī, the last day of the Durgā Pūjā (Kavikarṇapūra's *kāvya* XIX.5).

[54]The names of some of the queens are given below:

Chandrakalā—Jayānanda's *Chaitanya Maṅgal*
Bhānumatī—Īśvara Dāsa's *Chaitanya Bhāgavata*
Padmāvatī—*Saravatī Vilāsam* ascribed to Pratapa Rudra
Vidyukāntī—Sudarsana Dāsa's *Chaurāsi Ājnā*
Gaurī—Divākara Dāsa's *Jagannātha Charitāmṛita*

[55]*Chaitanya Chandrodaya* drama IX.22.

[56]*Ch. Ch.* II.16. Pichhaldā is situated on the southern bank of the Rupnarayan, about 13 miles from its confluence with the Hooghly.

the river till the conclusion of peace with the Yāvana king.[57] However, an Oriya servant of the Muslim military officer (Fauzdar) of the border area told him about the wonderful deeds of the ascetic coming from Orissa. This turned the mind of the Fauzdar who sent a Hindu officer to the frontier of Orissa to provide a safe escort.

But Chaitanya did not go to Vṛindāvana. Probably at Śāntipur, he met his mother. He went up to Rāmakeli (about 16 miles southeast of Malda, now in the Rajsahi district, Bangladesh) to meet two Hindu officers of the Sultan. Later on they became known as Rūpa and Sanātana. They advised the Master not to proceed further because of the hostile attitude of the Sultan of Bengal. Chaitanya also appreciated their frank criticism that it was not proper for a monk to go on pilgrimage to Vṛindāvana accompanied by a large number of followers.[58] Chaitanya returned to Puri after an absence of eight months before the chariot festival in 1515.

(xviii) *Journey to Vṛindāvana*

Chaitanya waited till the rains were over. He set out for Vṛindāvana in autumn of 1515. He stole away with only one attendant. He even avoided the road to Cuttack, and passed through a forest (Chandkā?) full of wild animals. Chaitanya probably followed an unfrequented path across the highlands of Mayurbhanj and passed through Jhārkhand in Bihar.

Kavikarṇapūra in his drama (IX.39-48) gives a vivid description of Chaitanya's visit to Vṛindāvana, which is associated with Kṛishṇa-legends. He fell into trances when he discovered the *Rādhā-kunda* (tank). Kṛishṇadās Kavirāj writes that his emotional ecstasy "was hundred times more intense than what it was at Nīlāchala." On his way back, he had learned disputations on Vedanta with some scholars at Vārānasi. During his return journey to Puri he followed the same lonely forest route through Jharkhand. He reached Puri after an absence of about ten months. He never left Puri during the last years of his life between 1516 and 1533.

(xix) *The last years of Chaitanya (1516-1533)*

The last years of Chaitanya's life at Puri may be divided into two phases. In the first few years he was quite normal. According to Kṛishṇadās Kavirāj, he punished junior Haridās for improper conduct. He had

---

[57] *Chaitanya Chandrodaya* drama IX.26. Kavikarṇapūra's statement shows that hostile relations between the two kingdoms continued even in 1514, though active fighting had ended by that time.

[58] *Murāri*, III.18.

theological discourses with Sanātana and Rāmānanda. He himself recited a śloka and explained its purport to Rāmānanda and Svarūpa Dāmodara.[59] He questioned Vallabha Bhaṭṭa's interpretation of the *Bhāgavata*, repudiating the commentary of Śrīdhar Svāmī. Chaitanya refused to intervene on behalf of Gopīnāth Patnaik, whom the king was going to punish for embezzlement. He even threatened to go away to Ālālnāth. Chaitanya sported with his companions in the tanks. The Master wanted to make Vṛindāvana, a missionary centre of his sect. He advised Rūpa and Sanātana to settle there and to write the doctrines of the faith. He also sent Raghunāth Bhaṭṭa, who became another Gosvāmī to Vṛindāvana. Like a worldly-person, he advised Jagadānanda, on his way to Vṛindāvana, not to travel beyond Vārānasi without an escort. Kṛishṇadās Kavirāj wanted to show the divine power of Chaitanya, even in eating, by making exaggerated statements.[60] The death of the pious Vaishṇava Haridās deeply moved the Master. The sight of Vṛindāvana had a lasting effect upon his mind. A state of quietism led to the realization of his true self. He began to experience with deepening emotion, transcendent love which made him oblivious of his earthly existence.

(xx) Love sickness of Chaitanya

During the last few years before his passing away, Chaitanya was love sick (*prema unmāda*) for Kṛishṇa.[61] He used to chant Kṛishṇa's name in solitude throughout nights on the sea coast.[62] At times overcome with grief, he wanted to put an end to his life by jumping into the sea.[63]

The Master went through the daily routines of his life through force of habit. He went to the Jagannāth temple early in the morning. He

---

[59]*Ch. Ch.* III.15.13. He also tested the knowledge of Rūpa Gosvāmī and appreciated the verses quoted by Rūpa (*Ch. Ch.* III.1.105 & 112).

[60]It is stated in the *Chaitanya Charitāmṛita* that though the Master lived on meagre meals as an ascetic (III.8), he sometimes obliged his followers who invited him to take meals in their houses by eating an enormous quantity of food. Thus Jagadānanda 'fed him tenfold'.

Chaitanya once dined at the house of Sārvabhauma. He ate a quantity of food, which in the opinion of Amogh (son-in-law of Sārvabhauma) "would have satisfied the appetite of ten or twelve persons" (II.15.248). Amogh was attacked with cholera (probably for making such disparaging statements). He would have died but for the grace of Chaitanya.

[61]While describing the love-sickness of Chaitanya, whom he depicted as the united form of Rādhā and Kṛishṇa, Kṛishṇadās Kavirāj had utilized Rūpa Gosvāmī's description of Rādhā's intense emotions due to her separation from Kṛishṇa, in the *Ujjvala Nīlamani*.

[62]*Ch. Bhāgavat*, III.3.410.

[63]Poem of Narahari Sarkar: *Padakalpataru* No. 832.

daily recited and counted the names of Hari and Kṛishṇa for several hours. Chaitanya also sang and danced before Jagannāth during the chariot festival. But his emotional fervour gradually grew in intensity. He was consoled according to his mood (*Bhāvānurupa*) by Rāmānanda's recitation of verses from the *Bhāgavata, Gīta Govinda* and from his own play *Jagannāth Vallabha* describing the pining of Rādhā and the Gopis for Kṛishṇa. Svarūp Dāmodar also sang songs from the *Śrī Kṛishṇa Kirtan* of Chaṇḍidās[64] and of Vidyāpati. He also quoted appropriate verses from the *Kṛishṇa Karṇāmṛita*. Chaitanya was mentally sedate enough to appreciate the verses and songs in Sanskrit.

Once while going to the Yameśvar Totā (garden) he heard a song from the *Gītā Govinda* being melodiously sung at some distance. Chaitanya ran in a frenzied state of mind in search of the singer. While he moved through the bushes his body was bruised by thorns. Fortunately, Govinda, who accompanied him, caught hold of him and told that the singer was a woman. Chaitanya regained his normal senses and thanked Govinda for saving him from contact with a woman.[65]

We have descriptions of Chaitanya's devotional ecstasy in the writings of contemporary persons. Raghunāth Dās Gosvāmī who was a companion of Chaitanya at Puri describes the emotions of the Master:

> "Let Lord Gaurāṅga appearing before my mind exuberate me. He, who accounts for the sincere delight of the Lord of the blue mountain (Nīlāchala) by way of smiling, perspiring and dancing: having had bedecked himself with nine varieties of gem; in the form of ever increasing change of complexion, tremors, tears and joy."[66]

It is stated in the *Chaitanya Chandrāmṛita* (verse 135) that "Lord Kṛishṇa in the form of Gaurāṅga sits on the sea shore; and having placed his cheek, as pale as the 'Badara' flower on his hands, is rendering the ground sprinkled with tears of his eyes."

Narahari Sarkar writes: "Gora Rāyā spends the night within the *Gambhirā* without sleep. At times he weeps, shouts out of grief or shivers. When he is alone, he rubs his face on the floor. Then, raising his hands,

---

[64]But Dr. Asit Banerjee writes that Chaitanya appreciated the poems on Rādhā-Kṛishṇa of another Chaṇḍidās.

Bangla Sāhityer Itibritta, Pt II, p. 631 (Calcutta, 1966).

[65]*Ch. Ch.* III.13.85.

[66]*Alankrityātmānaṃ Nava Vividha Ratnaraiba Bala*
Dvivarṇatva Stambhāsphuta Vachana Kampāsru Pulakaih
Hasan Svidyyannrityan Śitigiripate Nirbhara Mudē
Puraḥ Śrī Gauraṅgō Hṛidaya Udayanmāṃ Madayati
Stavakalpataru.

he laments for his beloved. Narahari says that his Gorā has become obsessed with the feeling of Rādhā."[67]

Occasionally he behaved like a frenzied person. Bāsu Ghosh writes:

> From the Lion gate, Gorā runs towards the sea, asking everybody, 'where is Kṛishṇa'? He is surrounded by his followers, chanting the name of Hari (to his ears). In the midst of the gathering, his body, having golden complexion, rolls on the ground. The tall figure of Gorā lies prostrate on the ground having lost consciousness. Foam comes out of his mouth. Vāsudeva Ghosh's heart is full of anguish, consequently.[68]

Kṛishṇadās Kavirāj refers to the *Stavakalpataru* V.8 in which Raghunāth Dās describes how Chaitanya mistook the Chatak hillock at Puri as the Govardhana hill at Vṛindāvana. On his way to the sea, he once looked at the Chatak hillock and mistook it to be the Govardhana hill. He ran towards it but after covering some distance Chaitanya suddenly became numb. He wanted to speak but could not pronounce a word due to excess of emotion. Flowing tears blinded his eyes. There was a quivering sensation throughout his body. He lost his senses and collapsed on the ground.[69]

Vṛindāvan Dās writes that once the Master, walking in a trance, fell into a well. He was picked up unhurt by his companions.[70] There is an interesting story in the *Chaitanya Charitāmṛita* (III.18) the source of which is not known. Kṛishṇadās Kavirāj writes that on one night the Master was walking on the sea coast. The sea waves sparkled in moonlight. The sight threw him into rapture. Thinking the sea to be the Yamunā, the Master ran into it. He was carried away by the sea waves towards Konarak. His unconscious body was recovered by a fisherman in his net. No other writer has mentioned this incident.

Towards the end of his life, Chaitanya was frequently under trance. He was now carefully watched day and night by his personal attendant Govinda. Svarūp Dāmodar and Raghunāth Dās were always present in Kāśi Miśra's house. Ray Rāmānanda constantly remained near Chaitanya to console him. It is stated by Kṛishṇadas Kavirāj, that on two nights the Master imagined that Kṛishṇa was playing flute and in a state of

---

[67] *Padakalpataru* No. 1463.

[68] *Padakalpataru* No. 1662.

[69] Similarly, Rūpa Gosvāmī writes that whenever the Master saw the groves on the sea coast, he was afflicted by the memory of Vṛindāvana (*Vṛindāraṇya smaraṅa janita prema vivaśāḥ*).

Chaitanyashṭaka I.6.

[70] *Chaitanya Bhāgavat* III.11.515.

semi-trance he left the cell, which was guarded at night by Govinda. The door for exit from the house was closed. Chaitanya miraculously left the house. His unconscious body was found near the main gate of the Jagannāth temple. We are told that on the first occasion, his body stretched to nine feet in length. Next time, his limbs had shrunk into his trunk and he looked like a tortoise. He was foaming at the mouth. The cows were smelling him. This incident has been mentioned by Raghunāth Dās Gosvāmi in his poem, *Stavakalpataru* verse V. Chaitanya behaved like a demented person, while constantly thinking of Kṛishṇa. Often he talked incoherently. Sometimes he shouted, laughed and wept senselessly. Due to emotional frenzy, he bruised his face by rubbing it violently on the floor. His frail body could not tolerate this constant torture and broke down finally.

CHAPTER IV

The Passing Away of Chaitanya

THE PASSING away of Chaitanya is shrouded in mystery.* The orthodox writers are silent about the date and the manner of his death. According to the Gauḍīya canons, Chaitanya is the incarnation of Kṛishṇa, and thus, any question of his death is *a priori* absurd. Kavikarṇapūra at the end of his poetical work *Chaitanya Charitāmṛita* simply informs that the Master returned to his celestial abode. Kṛishṇadās Kavirāj writes that the Master's disappearance (*Antārdhāna*) took place in Śaka 1455-1533 A.D.[1] There are four versions regarding the passing away of Chaitanya. It is stated that he passed away:

(1) In the garden-house adjacent to the Gopīnāth Temple.
(2) Within the Gopīnāth temple.
(3) In the Guṇḍichā house.
(4) In the Jagannāth temple.

In Jayānanda's *Chaitanya Maṅgal* we find the earliest reference to the death of Chaitanya. He writes that Chaitanya decided to go back to Vaikuṇṭha (Vishṇu's abode) on the seventh day of the full moon in the month of Āshādha.

> "While dancing before the chariots in the month of Āshādha, his left toe was pierced by a brick (lying on the road). . . . "On the sixth day, the pain in his toe became severe and he was forced to take shelter in the *Toṭā* (garden). He told Gadādhar Paṇḍit Gosvāmī that he would leave (the world) next night in the tenth hour". . . . "His material body lay behind, while he went to *Vaikuṇṭha* (Vishṇu's abode) in Vishṇu's chariot".[2]

---

*It may be a fact that he jumped into the sea in a fit of ecstatic emotion and disappeared for ever. But there is no literary evidence to corroborate this assumption.

[1] *Ch. Ch.* I.13.

[2] Jayānanda's *Chaitanya Maṅgal*, p. 150.

Jayānanda's statement is generally believed because it refers to a natural death. In his description of the passing away of Chaitanya, the embodiment of Kṛishṇa, in Āshādha, Jayānanda bears in mind the passing away of Kṛishṇa in the month of Āshādha. His foot was also pierced (by an arrow). Gadādhar Paṇḍit was the spiritual guide of Jayānanda. So Chaitanya was tended during his illness in the *Toṭā* of the Gopīnāth temple by Gadādhar.[3] Chaitanya was not taken to Kāśi Miśra's house, where he lived, and was attended by Svarūp Dāmodar, Ray Rāmānanda and Govinda.

In the beginning of the eighteenth century, Narahari Chakravarti in his *Bhakti Ratnākar* modified the statement of Jayānanda, which makes a blasphemous reference to Chaitanya's dead body. Instead of a natural death in the garden house adjacent to the Gopīnāth temple, he describes a miraculous disappearance within that temple. The Master was supposed to be the dual incarnation of Rādhā and Kṛishṇa. Thus a fitting end will be absorption within the image of Gopīnāth.

In the eighth canto of the *Bhakti Ratnākar*, Māmu Ṭhākur, the priest of the Gopīnāth temple, showed the site of Chaitanya's disappearance to Narottam. "Behold Narottam" he said "Here Gaurahari told something to (Gadādhar) Paṇḍit. . . . He entered into the temple of Gopīnāth. He vanished and never came out again." Narahari Sarkar's work is in the approved list of the Gauḍīya texts. These lines from the *Bhakti Ratnākar* are quoted on a marble slab in the wall of the Gopīnāth temple.

The conclusion is obvious. Though the orthodox Gauḍīya Vaishṇavas were at first reticent about any reference to the passing away of the Master, they had to modify their stand at least from the 18th century, to counteract the notion of absorption within Jagannāth. It also gave rise to a rhyme.

"What I shall say? Whither shall I go? Words are failing me (to describe the grief). I have lost Gorāchānd in the shrine of Gopīnāth."

Lochan Dās in his *Chaitanya Maṅgal* (p. 210) also mentions the seventh 'Tithi' (lunar day) of Āshādha, Sunday, to be the date of Chaitanya's passing away. He also accepts the Oriya tradition that Chaitanya absorbed himself into the image of Jagannāth.[4] So he writes

[3]There is reference to Chaitanya's passing away in the *Toṭā* Gopīnāth in the *Prema Taraṅgiṇi* (canto 36) by Sadānanda Kavisūrya Brahmā (*Ashṭachālisa barashe antardhana Toṭā Gopināthа sthāne*). Kavisurya Brahmā traces his spiritual descent from Gadādhar. There was a large *Toṭā* around the Yameśvar and the Gopīnāth temples. Kṛishṇadas Kavirāj calls it *Toṭa* Yameśvar (*Ch. Ch.* III.13). It is said that Chaitanya dug out the image of Gopīnāth from sand and gave it to Gadādhar Paṇḍit for worship. Gadādhar spent his last years in *Toṭa* Gopīnāth.

[4]In this description of Chaitanya as Kṛishṇa at Navadvīpa, Lochan treats his preceptor Narahari Sarkar *pari passu* with Gadādhar Paṇḍit (*Chaitanya Maṅgal* p. 3,

that Chaitanya passed away in the Guṇḍichā house where Jagannāth was staying at that time.

He writes that on that date, Chaitanya entered the Jagannāth temple. He looked all around but could not see Jagannāth. So with a heavy heart he quit that place. On Sunday noon, in the third 'prahara' the Master absorbed himself into the image of Jagannāth *(Jagannāthe līna Prabhu hailā āpane)*.

It is stated that the 'Parichhā' (Superintendent) of the Guṇḍichā temple rushed outside and told the devotees who were waiting there: "The Master has disappeared within the Guṇḍichā house! (*Guṇḍichā bāḍir madhye Prabhur haila antardhān*). I have personally witnessed the communion of Lord Gaura (and Jagannāth)!"

Lochan Dās failed to narrate the disposal of Chaitanya's body. Had the Master's body been brought out from the Guṇḍichā temple, the event would not have remained secret.

Among the Bengali writers, only Īśān Nagar in his *Advaita Prakāś* refers to the passing away of Chaitanya in the Jagannāth temple. According to some scholars it is an apocryphal work. Īśān Nagar says that Chaitanya one day went to the Jagannāth temple (*Śrī Mandir*). As he entered, the door of the temple got closed. After some time the door opened itself, but the Master was not to be seen. All guessed that the Master had disappeared. Thus in Bengal also, some Vaishṇavas believed that Chaitanya passed away in the Jagannāth temple. Contemporary persons at Puri like Ray Rāmānanda, Svarūp Dāmodar, Raghunāth Dās and Kānāi Khunṭiā do not refer to the passing away of Chaitanya in their writings.

Achyutānanda is the only eye-witness who has recorded the event. He writes in the *Śūnya Saṁhitā*:

> Gaurāṇga Chandra, after going round the exterior wall entered into the Temple (carrying the staff and water pot) with his followers. The Rājā was present there along with his councillors and ministers. While devotedly they were gazing at the image (of Jagannāth), the temple resounded with the name of Hari. "Lord Chaitanya, the great dancer, chanted the name of Rādhā and like a flash of lightning merged himself within the sacred body of Jagannāth.[5]

p. 13). He did not like to give prominence to Gadādhar by making the 'Toṭā Gopīnāth', the last resting place of Chaitanya. Though Lochan accepts the date mentioned by Jayānanda, he locates the passing away in the Guṇḍichā house. Lochan Dās had some knowledge of Orissa. He made a free translation of Rāmānanda's *Jagannāth Vallabha* drama.

[5] *Chaitanya Thākura mahā nṛityakāra Rādhā Rādhā dhvani kale*
Jagannāth Mahāprabhu śrī aṅge vidyuprāya miśi gale
Śūnya Saṁhitā—I.

The formless Brahma revealed himself from Void into the world to show his exploits. Destroying ignorance (i.e. darkness) and imparting knowledge of truth, he got absorbed into full manifestation of all the attributes (i.e. into Jagannāth). Just as fire, in swallowing fire, knows no check, similarly, (Chaitanya) the embodiment of celestial attributes, absorbed himself within a similar entity, before one could clearly visualize. Witnessing this (disappearance) the king broke into loud wailing and there was a general lamentation.

Achyutānanda has not mentioned the date of the passing away. He writes: "At day break, the Lord of the Universe (Jagannāth) was dressed for a festive occasion. From Mādhava full moon day, the king conducted a grand festival."

The word 'Mādhava' signifies the month of Vaiśākha. The festival conducted by the king seems to be the *Chandan Yātrā*, commencing from '*Akshaya Tritiyā*' which falls on the third day of the bright fortnight in the month of Vaiśākha.

Divākara Dāsa refers to Chaitanya's passing away as follows: "Thinking thus (that he should return to his own abode) he absorbed himself within the image of Jagannāth. Thus he vanished into Jagannāth's body (which is identical with his own) unperceived by all. The king was mad with consuming grief. "Master", he bewailed "You have disappeared."[6]

Īśvara Dāsa has vividly described the passing away of Chaitanya in his *Chaitanya Bhāgavata*. The Master decided to go back to Vaikuṇṭha when he reached the age of forty-eight. He consulted Advaita and Nityānanda in this connection. Īśvara Dāsa writes:

> "Thus passed several days and again befell the *Chandan Yātrā*. On the day of *Akshaya Tṛitiyā* Chaitanya decided to go to Vaikuṇṭha."[7] He joined the procession of the Vaishṇavas chanting the name of Hari on the main road. Advaita, Nityānanda, Vakreśvar, Hṛidayānanda, Gadādhar, Nānak and the five comrades accompanied him. The king was also present there. Getting near (the image of) Jagannāth, he beheld the Lord of the world. Chaitanya besmeared the sacred body (of Jagannāth) with sandal paste, and gazed at the Lord who illuminates the world.

---

[6] "*Emanta kahi Śrī Chaitanya*
Gopana hoile svadehe
Raja hoile mane chhanna
Śrī Jagannāth ange līna
Dehi kāhāra dṛisṭi nohe
He Prabhu hela antardhāna"
Jagannātha Charitāmṛita—Canto—7

[7] *Emante kichhi dina yāi*
Sedina ye yātrā Chandana
Akshaya Tṛitiyā dina hoi
Chaitanya Vaikuṇṭha gamana
Chaitanya Bhāgavata—Canto—64

Jagannāth stretched his hands and took the pot of sandal paste. He opened his mouth and Chaitanya got absorbed within him.[8]

We find that Achyutānanda, Divākara and Īśvara clearly state that Chaitanya passed away before the image of Jagannāth in the Jagannāth temple. Īśvara Dāsa categorically affirms that the Master's passing away took place on the *Akshaya Tritiyā* day. Even if we tentatively accept the date, we may enquire about the disposal of the body. The king of Sampurnanagara made similar enquiry in the *Chaitanya Bhāgavata.*

Hearing of the disappearance of Chaitanya into the sacred image, from the lips of the venerable sage Agastya, the king bowed down at his feet and exclaimed: "A strange fact you have related, O sage."

Then he put forward his query:

> "You say that Chaitanya while besmearing sandal paste, vanished into the sacred image. Thus Chaitanya merged his identity into Jagannāth's body. But what happened to the body of Chaitanya? I entertain doubt as to this. Briefly explain this to me and drive out misgiving from my mind."

The sage complied with the royal request. First of all, he explained that after fulfilling his mission, Chaitanya vanished into Jagannāth.

> "Chaitanya got absorbed into the god of the blue mountain. The form and spirit of Jagannāth and of Chaitanya are of identical nature. It was witnessed by all but nobody noticed what befell to the *illusory body*."[9]

Jagannāth, the fascinator of the three worlds, saw the body of Chaitanya from his throne. He ordered Kshetrapāla (an attendant deity)—'Anon shalt thou carry away the body in air, and place it on the water of the Gaṅgā'. At Jagannāth's bidding, Kshetrapāla carried away

---

[8]*Chandana khorā haste paḍi* *Sri Jagannātha bhuja bhidi*
Śrī mukha bistāri Gosāin *Garbhe Chaitanya līna hoi*

Chaitanya Bhāgavata—Canto—64 (University edition).

In my manuscript of the *Chaitanya Bhāgavata*, there is no reference to the taking of the pot by Jagannāth. It is stated: "The king personally witnessed the disappearance of Chaitanya (into Jagannāth). His indignation knew no bounds and despair filled his heart, getting composed, all (devotees) consoled Nityānanda."

[9]Jayānanda in his *Chaitanya Maṅgal* writes that Chaitanya's illusory body remained behind (*Māyā śarīr tathā rahila paḍiā*). But no other writer except Īśvara Dāsa has mentioned how the body of Chaitanya was disposed of after his passing away. There was a secret passage in the Jagannāth temple (*Mahābhāva Prakāśa* by Kānāi Khunṭiā—III). Chaitanya's body was probably taken out by that passage.

the dead body (*Śaba*) in air and immersed it on the water of the Gaṅgā.[10]

It is believed that the river Gaṅgā appears in the sacred river Prāchi (in the Puri district) at the Gomatī Tīrtha on the Akshaya Tṛitiyā day to clean herself, as she becomes impure by her contact with the sinners who bathe in the Gaṅgā.[11]

Both Īśvara Dāsa and Achyutānanda agree that Chaitanya disappeared into the image of Jagannāth in the month of Vaiśākhā. Thus we are of opinion that the Master passed away due to exuberance of emotion, while rubbing sandal paste on the body of Jagannāth, on the Akshaya Tṛitiyā night.

Īśvara Dāsa's description of the disposal of the body is believable. Had it been buried or burnt at Puri, the location could not have been kept secret. Chaitanya's body was not secretly thrown away into the sea, as it was not the custom. Haridās's dead body was given a sand-burial on the sea-coast. It appears probable that the body of Chaitanya was secretly carried out in midnight and immersed in water at a lonely place like the Gomatī Tīrtha, situated at a distance of about 26 miles from Puri.

Nonetheless, we should not categorically reject also the date, suggested by Jayānanda and Lochan Dās, long before Īśvara Dasa.[12] We can conclude that Chaitanya passed away before the image of Jagannāth, on a sunday, during the bright fortnight, either on the third *tithi* of Vaiśākha (27 April) or on the seventh *tithi* of Āshādha (29 June) in the year 1533.

---

[10]*Sehi svarūpa Śrī Chaitanya*
Śrī Jagannātha kalebara
Samaste emanta dekhanti
Chaitanya piṇḍa, siṁhāsana
Kshetrapālaṅku ājñā dei
Antarkhe nei Gaṅgā jala
Śrī Jagannātha ājñā pāi
Gaṅgāre meli dele Śaba
Lina ye Nilādri Lochana
Ekātmā ekāṅga śarīra
Māyā śarīra na jānanti
Dekhanti Trailokyamohana
'E piṇḍa nia bega karāi
Meliṇa dia Kshetrapāla'
Antarkhe nele Śaba bohi

Chaitanya Bhāgavata—Canto—65

[11]Uddhava Dāsā: *Prāchi Māhātmya*, canto XII (Cuttack 1921).

[12]It cannot be ruled out that Īśvara Dāsa deliberately chose an auspicious date for the passing away of Chaitanya. Jagannāth told Rājā Indradumnya 'Smear my body with sandal paste on the Akshaya Tṛitiyā day' (*Skanda Purāṇa*—Utkala Khaṇḍa—Canto 29).

CHAPTER V

Chaitanya and Jagannath

AFTER PUTTING on the robes of a monk, Chaitanya wanted to live in a forest for spiritual contemplation. Then he wanted to go to Vṛindāvana. But his followers took him to Śāntipur, where Advaita lived. Chaitanya stayed in Advaita's house for a few days and then he decided to go on pilgrimage to south India. He started for 'Jagannāth kshetra'.[1] After reaching Orissa, he expressed his eagerness to see the 'Lord of Nīlāchala'.[2]

At the first sight of the spire of the Jagannāth temple, he was overwhelmed with emotion and danced out of joy. He lost control of his senses when he beheld the image of Jagannāth seated on his dais.[3] The first *darśan* (sight) of Jagannāth had a lasting effect upon Chaitanya's mind. In a state of deep trance, he realized his indissoluble bond with the deity. His unconscious body was carried to Sārvabhauma's house. Next, when he visited the temple, the priests received him respectfully. They offered him *Prasāda* (oblations offered to a deity) which he received with great reverence.

Before Chaitanya went to the south, he visited the Jagannāth temple. The priests offered him the garland of the deity as a token of god-speed. Chaitanya returned to Puri before the Jyestha Purnima in 1512 to witness the Bath festival (*Snān-yātrā*).

Bath festival was followed by a period of '*anabasara*' (no time) when Jagannāth cannot be seen for fifteen days. Chaitanya went to Ālālnāth out of grief. Kṛishṇadās Kavirāj vividly describes the chariot festival which the Master witnessed for the first time. He saw with ecstatic joy the '*Pahaṇḍi vije*' ceremony after which the deities left the temple. He followed the images during the journey to their respective vehicles. After

[1]*Kavya* of Kavikarṇapūra XI.74.

[2]*Chaitanya Bhāgavat* III.2.8.

[3]Chaitanya said "I rushed to embrace Jagannāth. What happened afterwards, I do not remember." He declared: "In future, I shall behold Jagannāth from outside. shall not enter the sanctum but stand near the Garuḍa pillar" (*Chaitanya Bhāgavat* III.2.484).

Chaitanya Image at Banki

Chaitanya Image at Pratappur

circumambulating the chariots, Chaitanya prostrated before the vehicles and paid reverence to the deities. His devotional fervour was manifested by various psychological symptoms. His whole body seemed to be joyous and the hairs on his head stood on their ends. There was flow of tears from his eyes which was followed by foaming of the mouth and a running nose. He shouted in Oriya, '*Manimā*' (O, Lord) with hands raised above his head. He danced in frenzied delight. Nityānanda caught hold of him, whenever he was about to collapse on the ground.

Kṛishṇadās did not forget to introduce miracles. Suddenly, Jagannāth's chariot stopped, as if Jagannāth wanted to witness the *kirtana* by Chaitanya and his followers. His chariot stuck in mud and even huge elephants could not move it. Chaitanya pushed the chariot with his head, and immediately the ponderous vehicle began to move.[4] A few days before the arrival of the deities in the Guṇḍichā-house, Chaitanya and his followers had swept and cleaned it by pouring hundreds of buckets of water. So long the deities were in the Guṇḍichā house, Chaitanya went there regularly and performed *kirtana*. Chaitanya participated in the Nandotsava festival, which followed Janmāshṭami, Kṛishṇa's birth day. At the command of the king, Tulsi Parichha, a temple servitor, tied the cloth of Jagannāth on the head of the Master[5]—which was the highest honour shown by the king of Orissa to an individual.

Kṛishṇadās Kavirāj gives another description of the chariot festival, in which Chaitanya participated after his return from Vṛindavāna. Out of excessive joy, he roared and leapt in front of the chariot of Jagannāth and frequently fainted. Due to overwhelming emotion, he could not even utter '*Jay* (glory to) Jagannāth'. He could only articulate 'Ja, Ja, Ga, Ga'. He remembered an Oriya song, which he asked Svarūp Dāmodar to recite.[6] The Master used to attend all festivals of Jagannāth with rapturous devotion. Even during the decade of love sickness, his daily routine, due to habit, was to go to the Jagannāth temple early in the morning for the *darśan* of Jagannāth.

Chaitanya considered Jagannāth to be Kṛishṇa himself. Whenever

---

[4]*Ch. Ch.* II.14.53.

"The Jagannāth temple symbolizes Dvāraka, where Jagannāth's (Kṛishṇa's) consorts reside; while the temple Guṇḍichā stands for Vraja (Vrindāvana) the abode of the Gopīs. The significance of the Car festival is that Jagannāth-Krishṇa goes to meet the Gopīs headed by Rādha.' N.N. Law: *Sri Krishna and Sri Chaitanya*, p. 52 (Luzac & Co. London 1949).

[5]*Ch. Ch.* III.15.29.

[6]*Ch. Ch.* III.10. Kṛishṇadās Kavirāj has quoted only the first line of the Oriya song *Jagamohana parimuṇḍā yāi* (Humbly, I do obeisance to Jagannāth). The word Jagamohana implies Jagannāth. Balarāma Das wrote the *Jagamohana Rāmāyana* in honour of Jagannāth. In the 18th century, Kṛishṇadāsa used the words *parimuṇḍa yāi*, now obsolete, in his poem *Deula Tolā*.

he saw the deity he imagined him to be Kṛishṇa at Kurukshetra. On one occasion he exclaimed: "Blessed is my life. I see my Lord today. His eyes are as beautiful as full blown lotus." He once addressed Jagannāth: 'Here am I and here you are and the joy of our union is ever new as of old.'

Kṛishṇadās narrated two incidents which show Chaitanya's devotion to Jagannāth. One day, the Master went to the Jagannāth temple and stood close to the Garuḍa pillar for the *darśan* of Jagannāth. An Oriya woman was unable to see the deity on account of the crowd. She climbed on the pillar for a clear vision of Jagannāth and rested one foot on a shoulder of the Master. Soon she realized her mistake and fell at Chaitanya's feet. The Master exclaimed, "This woman was so much absorbed in her passionate longing for Jagannāth that she failed to notice that she was standing on my shoulder. She is blessed. Let me worship her so that I may have the intensity of her devotion."[7]

Kṛishṇadās refers to another incident. On one occasion during his love sickness, Chaitanya went to the Jagannāth temple and searched for Kṛishṇa. The Pratihāri at the Lion gate bowed to the Master. Chaitanya held his hands and asked him to show Kṛishṇa. The Pratihāri took him inside the temple and both stood by the side of the Garuḍa pillar. The Pratihāri showed him Jagannāth and said, 'Here is your Kṛishṇa'. The Master imagined that Jagannāth was playing flute. And he was over-joyous.[8] Twice at night, in his trance, Chaitanya thought that the day had dawned. He moved out of his cell to visit Jagannāth. His unconscious body was found near the main gate of the Jagannāth temple.

Chaitanya was believed to be living (sachala) embodiment of Jagannāth.[9] Similarly, in Oriya *Chaitanya Bhāgavata* by Īśvara Dāsa canto 46, it has been stated that 'Gaurānga is Jagannāth himself'.

We will now refer to some eye-witnesses. Rūpa Gosvāmī spent ten months at Puri. In the seventh stanza of the first '*Chaitanyāshṭaka*' he refers to the Master's dance in front of the chariot of Jagannāth.[10]

Another eye-witness was Raghunāth Dās Gosvāmī. In the sixth verse of his poem '*Chaitanyāshṭaka*' he refers to the Master's *darśan* of

[7] *Ch. Ch.* III.14.

[8] *Ch. Ch.* III.16.

[9] *Chaitanya Bhāgavat* III.5.185.

[10] *Rathārudha Syārādadhi-Padabi Nīlāchalapate*
Badabhra Premormisphurita Naṭanollāsa Vivaśaḥ
Saharsham Gāyadbhiḥ Paribṛita Tanur-Vaishṇava Janaiḥ
Sa Chaitanyaḥ Kiṁ mẹ Punarapi Dṛiśoryyāsati Padaṁ

"Will ever again Chaitanya favour me with a sight of his person rendered senseless n exuberance of dancing, inspired by his boundless waves of devotion in front of the chariot ridden by the Lord of Nīlāchala and encircled by the Vaishṇavas singing in delight."

Jagannāth from the Garuḍa pillar.[11]

Dr. D.C. Sen writes: 'For eighteen years, Chaitanya stood by the side of the Garuḍa pillar resting his elbow on it for hours. From there he did not dare to go further near the temple lest the sight of the image would madden him with joy, as it had done him once, making him run in an unconscious state to the very pedestal of the image and embrace it."[12]

If we accept the Oriya version, Chaitanya passed away before the image of Jagannāth on the *Akshaya Tṛitiyā* night while smearing paste on the body of the deity. He resisted the temptation to approach Jagannāth for eighteen years. That night he could not control himself with fatal consequence.

Narahari Sarkar, another contemporary writer, gives a graphic description of Chaitanya's longing for Kṛishṇa when he behold Jagannāth. He writes:

> Gorā (Chaitanya was called Gaurānga or Gorā) beholds the Lord of Nīlāchala along with his associates. He becomes imbued with the feelings of the Gopīs. Bitterly he says 'I am pining for you, but you do not care for me! You had put me in the snare of love. Now, you are not to be seen. Thus laments Gorā with eyes full of tears.[13]

In the *Sri Krishṇalīlā* of Sanātana, there is a verse in adoration of Jagannāth in which Sanātana describes the deity as 'Chaitanya *Vallabha*'.

A scholar from east Bengal composed a drama on the life of Chaitanya and gave the script to Svarūp Dāmodar with the hope that he might read a portion of the script before the Master. In the *Nandi* sloka (introductory verse) the poet compared Chaitanya with Jagannāth. He wrote: 'Jagannāth has a beautiful form and Chaitanya is the embodiment of that form in real life. That is: Jagannāth is a wooden image and Chaitanya is like the soul of that image. Chaitanya has manifested himself to infuse consciousness in Jagannāth's image, which is an inanimate object.' After hearing the ṣloka, Svarūp Dāmodar rejected the manuscript as heretical. It is now lost. Svarūp Dāmodar found that in the *Nandi*

---

[11]Puraḥ *Paśyan Nīlāchalapati Muru Prema Nivahaiḥ Ksharannetrāmbhobhiḥ Snapita Nija Dīrghojjvala Tanuh Sadā Tiṣṭhan Deśe Pranayī Garuḍa Sṭambha Charame Śaichī Sūnuh kim me Nayana Śaranīṃ Yāsyati Punah?*

"Will ever again the son of Śachī favour me with an appearance within my view, standing as he always did, on a site near his favourite pillar of Garuḍa—the son of Śachī whose tall and lustrous body was drenched with the tears of his dripping eyes, due to increasing devotion, having had a sight of the Lord of Nīlāchala in front."

[12]D.C. Sen: *Chaitanya and His companions*, p. 231. On that occasion Chaitanya was unconscious for several hours. The Master admitted "Luckily I did not embrace Jagannāth. It would have caused peril (*sankaṭa*) to me. (*Chaitanya Bhāgavat* III.2)

[13]*Padakalpataru* (ed. by Satish Ch. Roy) No. 799.

sloka, Chaitanya has been made superior to Jagannāth. This would be resented by the Oriya Vaishṇavas and would also cause great annoyance to the Master.[14]

There is an interpolated verse in the *Garuḍa Purāṇa:* 'Lakshmikānta will manifest himself in the Kaliyuga. He will appear before Dāruḥ Brahma as an ascetic named Gaura'.

Kavikarṇapūra describes Chaitanya's devotion to Balarāma.[15] Chaitanya did not want to leave Puri. In 1514, he came back from Bengal. Next year he went to Vṛindāvana but did not stay there in spite of its association with the legends of Rādhā-Kṛishṇa. Nor did he return to Bengal. The result was that "the movement grew and expanded somewhat haphazardly in Bengal."[16]

It is not a fact that Chaitanya did not go back to Bengal because it was a Muslim country. Nityānanda and Advaita spread the Chaitanya faith in Bengal introducing *Guruvāda* (worship through the medium of a Guru or preceptor). They were not molested by the Muslim kings, or their officers.[17] Husain Shah's army invaded Orissa and destroyed some Hindu temples in the enemy country, but the Muslim kings did not stop the annual pilgrimages of their Hindu subjects to Puri.

Chaitanya's attachment to Jagannāth defies rational explanation. Kavikarṇapūra writes that the Master spent twenty years out of his ascetic life of twenty-four years, in witnessing the festivals at Śrīkshetra (Puri).[18] It is stated in the *Jagannātha Charitamṛita*, III by Divākara Dāsa that the Gauḍīya devotees of Chaitanya asked him to leave Puri and to visit other holy places. Hearing this, Chaitanya said: 'With all my mental attitude and intelligence, I have taken shelter in Jagannāth. Whether I live or die, I cannot leave Jagannāth and go elsewhere.'

The grove on the sea coast, the sparkling sea waves, the Chatak hillock brought to his mind the memory of Vṛindāvana. But Chaitanya did not go there again. During his last days, he sent Jagadānanda to Vṛindāvana, but did not express desire to accompany him. In spite of his devotion, Chaitanya did not compose any *stotra* in honour of Jagannāth.[19]

---

[14]But in the *Chaitanya Chandrodaya* drama (Act VIII) Chaitanya has been described as '*Nara Brahma*' (human embodiment of Brahma) and Jagannāth as '*Dāru Brahma*' (wooden embodiment of Brahma).

[15]*Chaitanya Charitāmrita kāvya* XIII.56.

[16]De, op. cit. p. 105.

[17]Husain Shah encouraged Parameśvara to translate the Sanskrit *Mahābhārata.* Vijaya Gupta praises Husain Shah in his *Padma Purāna* for the Sultan's patronage.

[18]*Kavya*, XX.40.

[19]There is a hymn, dubiously ascribed to Chaitanya, known as '*Jagannāth Ashṭaka*' praying Jagannāth to appear before his vision. The first stanza of this hymn is quoted below:

Kadāchit Kālindi Taṭa Bipina Saṅgitaka Baro

Even when he witnessed Jagannāth for the first time on the chariot in 1512, he repeatedly recited a verse in adoration of Kṛishṇa at Kurukshetra.[20]

Mudābhīrī Narī Badana Kamalāsvāda Madhupaḥ
Ramā Śambhū Brahmā Surapati Ganeśārchita Pado
Jagannātha Svāmī Nayanapatha Gāmī Bhavatu Me

May Lord Jagannāth, who is skilled in producing music, and who, once upon a time in the forests on the banks of the Yamunā, had the pleasure of tasting like a bee, the lotus-like faces of the cowherd women; and whose feet are worshipped by goddess Lakshmī, gods Śiva, Brahmā, Indra and Gaṇeśa; come to my sight.

In some manuscripts, the first line of the verse differs. In at least two manuscripts, the poem contains ten, instead of eight stanzas and is called *Jagannāth Daśaka.* Sibchandra Seal: *Bangiya Sahitya Parishad Patrika*, Bengali year 1331-1924 AD, p.89.

[20]Kṛishnadās Kavirāj writes that the feeling of Chaitanya at the sight of Jagannāth was similar to that of Rādhā when she saw Kṛishṇa at Kurukshetra. There he wore royal dress and was surrounded by horses, elephants as well as by a large gathering of people. But she longed for Kṛishṇa, dressed as a cowherd, in the secluded groves of Vṛindāvana.

Rūpa Gosvāmī composed a verse (*Padyāvali* No. 383) at Puri, describing Radha's longing at Kurukshetra, which received the approval of Chaitanya (*Ch. Ch.* II.1.76).

APPENDIX

Chaitanya as an Embodiment of Buddha-Jagannath

JAYDEVA IN his *Gītā-Govinda* described Buddha as the ninth incarnation of Vishṇu. An *Ādi* or Primordial Buddha rather than human Buddha fitted well with the conceptions of the Fish, Tortoise and Boar incarnations. Jagannāth was gradually conceived as Ādi Buddha and the ninth incarnation of Vishṇu.

The conception of Jagannāth as the embodiment of Buddha appealed to the imagination of Sāralā Dās, who wrote the *Mahābhārata* in Oriya in the 15th century. He writes 'To deliver mankind, Jagannāth has manifested in the form of Buddha.'[21]

Kṛishṇa reappeared as Ādi Buddha Jagannāth after his passing away. According to the tradition narrated in the *Dāru Brahma Gītā* ascribed to Jagannāth Dās, one of the five Associates, the Pāṇḍavas arranged for the cremation of Kṛishṇa's body. Only the hands and legs were consumed by fire. "To assume the form of Buddha, the Lord gave up His hands and legs." The divine oracle was then heard to cast the unburnt portion of the body into the sea which would appear as '*Dāru Brahma*' on the sea coast at Nīlāchala. Thus Jagannāth is Kṛishṇa.[22] Many Oriya Vaishṇavas believed that Chaitanya was the partial manifestation of Jagannāth-Buddha and he was absorbed within Jagannāth after the completion of his mission. The Lord (Kṛishṇa) told Sudāma (who was reborn as Achyutānanda) that He would appear in His Buddha incarnation in the Kaliyuga. 'My partial manifestation will appear at Navadvīpa and be known as Chaitanya.'[23]

In the *Chaitanya Bhāgavata* by Īśvara Dāsa, Chaitanya has been described as the Buddha incarnation at the end of each colophon

---

[21]*Baudha rupare bije achhi Jagannātha*—Sabhā Parva.

[22]Achyutānanda writes in his *Śūnya Saṃhitā*, XXX, that Hari (Kṛishṇa) incarnating himself as Buddha would enjoy majestic splendour. Elsewhere, in the same canto he writes that Hari manifests himself 'in the form of Buddha at Nīlāchala' (*Baudha rupare Nīlāchale acchi rahi*).

[23]*Śūnya Saṃhitā*, X.

(*Bodhāvatāra*). The Lord said "I am Chaitanya in the form of Buddha."[24] "The holder of the conchshell (Krishna) in his Buddha incarnation has revealed himself as Chaitanya."[25]

---

[24] "*Bolanti Prabhu Bhagavānà Baudha rupa mna Chaitanya*"
Chaitanya Bhāgavata—canto 46

[25] *Buddha rupe Kambudhara Chaitanya svarupe vihāra*
Chaitanya Bhāgavata—canto 48

CHAPTER VI

Religious Outlook of Chaitanya

CHAITANYA'S DEVOTION was broad-based and liberal. He was above the sectarian spirit of exclusiveness. The Master declared that a person, even if he be a Śūdra, is a true Vaishṇava, if he recites the name of Kṛishṇa.[1] One of his intimate associates was Yāvana Haridās. Chaitanya worshipped Ambuliṅga Śiva and Jaleśvara Śiva on his way to Jajpur. Lōchan Dās writes in his *Chaitanya Maṅgal* (part two) 'Jajpur is full of Śiva images. Lord Gaurāṅga visited each of them. With joyful heart, he went to behold the goddess Virajā. In the bliss of gazing, love welled up and the Master prayed to Virajā for imparting devotion to his mind.' In his work, Murāri Gupta describes Chaitanya's visits to the Śiva temples at Bhubaneswar (canto VII). He danced and sang before Liṅgarāja Śivaliṅga.

Chaitanya revered all incarnations of Vishṇu. He praised Murāri Gupta for his poem '*Rāmāshaṭaka*' in praise of Rāma.[2] Murāri and Kavikarṇapūra write that the Master, on his way to the south, recited a poem invoking Kṛishṇa-Keśava and Rāma-Rāghava to protect him. Chaitanya visited the temple of Kūrma at Srikurmam and the temple of Nrisiṃha at Simhachalam. He frequently went to the temple of Ālālnāth or Alwārnāth.

The Master was a devotee of Gopāla-Kṛishṇa. He received initiation in Gopāla mantra from Īśvara Puri. He worshipped Gopāla (also called Gopīnāth) at Remuna and also Sākshi Gopāla (Gopala the witness) at Cuttack. When he first saw the spire of the Jagannāth temple from some distance, he recited with joy a verse: 'Behold the image of Bāla

---

[1] *Ch. Ch.* II. 8 & 18

[2] Vṛindāvan Dās: *Chaitanya Bhāgavat*: III.4.317. At Ramesvaram he worshipped Rāmeśvara Śiva which was installed by Rāmachandra. (Kavikarṇapūra's *kāvya* XIII.32).

The Master was imbued with the feeling of Hanumāna, the great devotee of Rāmachandra, on the *Vijayadaśami* day (*Ch. Ch.* II.15).

Gopāla, looking at me with smiling face from the top of the spire.'[3]

CHAITANYA AS THE FOUNDER OF A SECT

S.K. De writes that Chaitanya, due to his emotional absorption, had no time or willingness to found a sect.[4] He points out:

> At Benares, as well as at Puri, Chaitanya is represented by Kṛishṇadās Kavirāj as giving elaborate instructions to Sanātana and Rūpa in the dogmas and doctrines of the cult; but the six long chapters of the biography which are devoted to this detailed theological exposition merely gives a direct summary with free quotations, of the learned works which the two brothers themselves composed later on.[5]

Writing after about a century, Kṛishṇadās Kavirāj, in his excessive zeal, has drawn liberally from the *Bhaktirasāmrita Sindhu* of Rūpa and the *Brihad Bhāgavatāmṛita* of Sanātana in those chapters stated above. Nevertheless, it will not be wrong to presume that the Master imparted to Rūpa and Sanātana, the doctrinal foundation of his conception of the Rādhā-Kṛishṇa cult, during his close contact with them. It is not true that Chaitanya gave up scholastic pursuits and spent his time in the chanting of the name of Kṛishṇa. This wrong information comes from the fact that he composed nothing except a few verses in adoration of Kṛishṇa and eight verses called '*Sikshāsṭaka*'.

At Varanasi, where he met Sanātana, he had long theological discourses with Vedantic scholars. Even during the last decade of his life, when Chaitanya was subjected to hysterical emotions, he was consoled by recitations from the *Bhāgavata*, the *Jagannāth Vallabha* ḍrama and from the *Gita Govinda*.

According to S.K. De: 'Chaitanya never thought it necessary to emulate the examples of the founders of other Vaishṇava sects in the writing of religious or speculative works himself; nor did he care much about putting together all that he taught and practised.' But S.K. De admits that the theological works of Rūpa and Sanātana were 'probably directly inspired by his personal example and teaching'.[6]

It has already been pointed out that the two Gosvāmī brothers systematized the basic tenets of the faith which were expounded by

---

[3]*Chaitanya Bhāgavat* (III.2), 410.

[4]Jadunath Sarkar agrees with Dr. De's opinion and writes that 'Chaitanya did not found a church' (*History of Bengal*; Vol. II p. 220).

[5]S.K. De: *History of the Vaishnava Faith and Movement*, p. 100.

[6]De: op. cit., pp. 116-117.

Chaitanya himself. The question is, why did Chaitanya select them to be the chief theoreticians of the faith in preference to his favourite disciples at Navadvīpa and Puri? The Master wanted that a law-giver of the faith should be well-versed in his conception of the Kṛishṇa cult which gives prominence to Rādhā. He should be a person of austere character and live the life of a spiritual recluse to draw inspiration.[7]

The Master searched for suitable persons who could be entrusted with the task of writing the canonical works of the faith. Chaitanya's choice fell upon the two brothers Rūpa and Sanātana, which shows that he retained his power of judgement. They were ministers of Sultan Husain Shah. Sanātana had written to the Master, expressing the desire of the two brothers to become his disciples. Chaitanya had already sent Lokanāth, a monk, to Vṛindāvana to reclaim the holy sites. He now went to Rāmakeli which was the family seat of Rūpa and Sanātana. They were erudite theologians—predisposed to the worship of Kṛishṇa.[8] Chaitanya met Rūpa and Sanātana and selected them for the mission.

The Puri disciples

It is surprising that the Master did not consider his disciples at Puri, with whom he spent about twenty years of his ascetic life to be competent to write the doctrinal theology. Rāmānanda and Vāsudeva Sārvabhauma were accomplished scholars, but they were devoted to household affairs. It is stated in the *Chaitanya Charitāmṛita* that Chaitanya once said that Svarūp Dāmodar knew more about theology than he himself did (III. 6). But only a few ślokas of Svarūp Dāmodar have been found. Thus Chaitanya's statement befitting Vaishṇava humility does not prove the erudition of Svarūp Dāmodar.

Only Raghunāth Das, the writer of the *Stavāvali* and the *Vilāpa Kusumāñjali* could have been entrusted with that laborious work. His life is a unique example of sacrifice for attaining religious merit. 'Wealth equalling that of Indra, and a wife as beautiful as an Apsara' could not bind him to the worldly life. He settled at Puri and often lived on stale food which was thrown away by the Jagannāth temple pilgrims. He was

[7]While Nityānanda, the chief disciple of Chaitanya, renounced the life of hard asceticism, Rūpa and Sanātana preferred to be hermits. They gave up wealth and power to propagate the faith. The Master was happy when Sanātana gave away his blanket—the last article of luxury which he possessed.

[8]*Murāri* III.8. Rūpa and Sanātana disposed of their wealth. (*Chaitanya Chandrodaya* IX.45). Rūpa left Bengal and met the Master at Prayaga. Sanātana was imprisoned by the Sultan. But he managed to escape and arrived at Varanasi during Chaitanya's stay at that place.

probably lacking in personality. Raghunāth was overshadowed by his mentor Svarūp Dāmodar so long he was at Puri. His non-Brahman birth also disqualified him.

THE NAVADVIPA DISCIPLES

In 1512, Chaitanya returned from the south and finally decided to settle at Puri. Nityānanda accompanied him during his first journey to Puri and waited there for two years. Chaitanya requested him to go back to Bengal and to preach *Prema bhakti* (devotion based on love) to the people. He also sent back Advaita who had come to Puri.

Nityānanda again came to Puri to see the Master. He was once more requested by Chaitanya not to come to Puri 'but to fulfil his mission in Gauḍa.'[9] Nevertheless, Nityānanda at least once again came to Puri after the Master's return from Vṛindāvana.[10] Why did Chaitanya ask Nityānanda not to come to Puri? The propagation of the faith in Bengal would not have suffered because of Nityānanda's absence for a few months. It appears that Chaitanya apprehended that Nityānanda's somewhat unconventional life might be misunderstood in the temple-city.[11]

Nityānanda had a more liberal outlook than Chaitanya. He was an *Avadhuta* (monk who was not ordained) before he joined the Vaishṇava community at Navadvīpa. He was consequently not fastidious about the caste regulations. After his return to Bengal, he spread the faith by giving initiation to all classes of men. But the Master had respect for the existing social order.[12] At Puri, he did not want to defy the customs and the prejudices of the priests.[13] Complaint reached Chaitanya about Nityānanda's conduct after his return to Bengal. "Instead of the robes of a mendicant, he (Nityānanda) had put on silk garments, wore sandal

---

[9]*Ch. Ch.* II.16.64.

[10]On the last occasion, Nityānanda displayed unaccommodating temper. Nityānanda was coming to Orissa along with Sibānanda Sen, his family and some more pilgrims. Śivānanda, who acted as the guide, could not procure in one place food for the party. Nityānanda was hungry. He kicked Śivānanda and cursed that his three sons would die (*Ch. Ch.* III.12). Sivānanda kept quiet though his wife protested.

[11]Dr. Sukumar Sen: *Bangala Sāhit, ver Itihās* Vol. I p. 288.

[12]As Rāmānanda says: "Devotion to Vishnu can be attained only by performing the prescribed duties of the religion" *Ch. Ch.* II.8.

[13]Two of the greatest Vaishṇavas of the Chaitanya faith, Rūpa and Sanātana lived with Yāvana Haridās when they came to Puri, as they were considered to be defiled because of their close association with the Muslim king of Bengal. They kept away from the Jagannāth temple (*Ch. Ch.* III.4). Chaitanya did not object as their admission into the temple might have encountered opposition from the temple priests.

garlands and indulged in luxury."[14] Once a celibate, he simultaneously married two nieces of Gauridās Paṇḍit (Miśra), one of his close associates.

Though it is said that Nityānanda married with the consent of Chaitanya, there is no evidence to justify such an assumption. The Master thought that spiritual advancement was not possible for a worldly-minded person. Otherwise he would not have left his home, abandoning his old mother and young wife. Chaitanya did not advise Raghunāth Das to go back to Bengal, where he had left behind his parents and wife. Like Nityānanda, Advaita and Śrīvās were householders. So Chaitanya did not select them.

Gaudiya Vaishnavism

The Chaitanya faith is generally known as Bengal or Gauḍīya Vaishṇavism.[15] The Master spent his life as an ascetic mostly at Puri in Orissa. He made Vṛindāvana, and not Navadvīpa, the chief seat of his faith. Some of the prominent Vaishṇavas of the Chaitanya faith did not belong to Gauḍadeśa. Gopāla Bhaṭṭa, a Tamil Brahman, wrote the *Haribhakti Vilāsa*—the most important treatise on the ritual worship of the Chaitanya faith. Ray Rāmānanda, an Oriya, made significant contribution to the theology of the Chaitanya faith. Baladeva Vidyabhushan, another Oriya, affiliated the Chaitanya faith to the Mādhva sect. He also wrote the commentary on the *Vedānta Sūtra*, following the examples of other Vaishṇava sects.

Moreover, the religions, and in many cases the sects, are named after the founders, and not after the countries to which they belonged. The sect founded by Madhva, is not called Karṇāṭaka Vaishṇavism. The divinization of Nityānanda and the hereditary preceptorship are the features of the Navadvīpiya school in Bengal, or Gaudiya Vaishṇavism.

The Chaitanya faith can be appropriately called 'Gaurīya' (founded by Gaura or Gaurāṅga) Vaishṇavism.

Relation of Chaitanya with Orissan Vaishnavism

Chaitanya had many followers who did not accept the doctrines of his faith. Achyutānanda, who describes the concept of *Nirākāra* (formless)

[14]*Ch. Bhāgavat* III.6.19.

[15]In the 16th century, South-east Bengal was called Baṅgadeśa (*Ch. Ch.* III.5). The rest of Bengal was called Gauḍadeśa and the inhabitants were called Gauḍiya (*Ch. Ch.* II.11). Kavikarṇapūra refers to Gaudiya *bhāshā* (language) in the *Ch. Chandrodaya*, VII.

Kṛishṇa and gives a demonstration of the theory of Void claims to be his disciple.[16] This was possible because of the following reasons.

1. The congregation of the devotees of Chaitanya at Puri consisted of all Vaishṇavas, irrespective of sectarian distinctions who chanted the name of Hari.
2. *Kirtana*, specially before the chariot of Jagannāth, has an emotional appeal to all Oriya Vaishṇavas.
3. His God-dedicated personality and his devotional fervour at the sight of Jagannāth, impressed the Vaishṇavas of Orissa, who took him to be the embodiment of Jagannāth.
4. Lastly, it was believed that Chaitanya was an accomplished scholar, who had authoritative knowledge of the scriptures.[17]

---

[16]The conception of formlessness is repugnant to the tenets of the Chaitanya faith. As the Master told Sārvabhauma: 'The Supreme Being is full of powers, and yet you describe Him as formless. The Shrutis that speak of him as abstract, exclude the natural and set up the unnatural.'

Ch. Charitāmṛita—II.16

[17]*Mahā Paṇḍita ye Chaitanya Gossāin Veda Vedāntare sāra*

Śūnya Saṃhitā—I.

CHAPTER VII

Chaitanya's Association with Five Comrades

ACHYUTANANDA WRITES that the five associates, Jagannātha, Balarāma, Achyutānanda, Yaśovanta, and Ananta participated in the *kirtana* processions of Chaitanya. The last four were non-Brahmans. The first half of the sixteenth century was a period of religious ferment in Orissa. Non-Brahman religious teachers asserted the right of the non-Brahmans to take part in religious discourses along with the Brahmans and to read the scriptures. They translated the Sanskrit religious works into Oriya to make them available for the masses. They expounded mystical esoteric dogmas and gave demonstrations of their occult knowledge.

(i) PANCHA SAKHA CONNOTATION

The word 'Pañcha Sakhā' implies comradeship of five persons. But apart from Achyutānanda and Ananta (in *the Rāsa* manuscript attributed to him) other three, namely Balarāma, Jagannātha and Yaśovanta, do not refer to the connotation 'Pañcha Sakhā' or to their comradeship in their writings. Only in two other works, the *Chaitanya Bhāgavata* and the *Chaurāśī Ājñā*, there are references to 'Pañcha Sakhā'. Divākara gives the life history of Balarāma Dāsa in his *Jagannātha Charitāmṛita* but is silent about other comrades.[1] The question is: why did Achyutānanda use the word 'Pañcha Sakhā' when there is no clear evidence that they were intimate friends: though they might have known each other. The answer lies in the study of the religious history.

The Gauḍiya Vaishṇavas believe that Chaitanya is the embodiment of Kṛishṇa. The love-sickness of the Master during the last decade of his life and his passing away before the image of Kṛishṇa-Jagannāth spread that belief among the Vaishṇavas of Orissa. The word 'Sakhā' has a theological implication. In Orissa and Bengal, the disciples of

[1]Surendra Mohanty: *Oḍiyā Sāhityara Madhya parva* p. 218.

Chaitanya were conceived as associates (*gaṇa*) of Kṛishṇa in Vṛindāvana—'an extremely logical development of the Vaishṇava theory of incarnation which regards not only Chaitanya as Kṛishṇa, but also his followers as Kṛishṇa's associates and beloved ones'.[2]

Achyutānanda writes that Nīlakaṇṭheśvara Śiva of Puri consoled Kṛishṇa before his passing away: Nīlakaṇṭheśvara informed Kṛishṇa that his companions Dāma, Sudāma, Śrīvatsa, Suvala and Suvāhu would be born in the Kali yuga and would be named Ananta, Achyutānanda, Jagannātha, Balarāma, and Yaśovanta respectively.[3] Thus, we are told that the five comrades were the companions of Kṛishṇa in the Dvāpara Yuga and were born again to serve him.[4]

(ii) The concepts of five and twelve

'Pañcha' (five) has no special significance. Achyutānanda probably liked to use it to determine the number of comrades.[5] Likewise, in the third quarter of the sixteenth century, the conception of twelve Gopālas (associates of Kṛishṇa) became popular in Bengal. Gaurīdas Paṇḍit was considered to be Suvala in the Dvāpara Yuga.[6] The word 'Gopāla' was first used to denote the select disciples of Nityānanda.[7] Achyutānanda introduced the conception of 'Sakhā' to indicate that the five comrades were companions of Kṛishṇa.[8]

(iii) Chaitanya and the five comrades

According to Achyutānanda: 'Twelve thousand followers including the Pañcha Sakhā participated in the *kirtana* processions of the Master. The

---

[2]De: *History of Vaishnava Faith and Movement*, p. 45 fn.

[3]*Śūnya Saṁhitā*—Canto 27.

[4]*Śūnya Saṁhitā*—I and XI.

[5]In the *Śūnya Saṁhitā*, there are references to the number Five:

(1) 'Vargas'—Symbols—These are sketched during the Void worship.

(2) 'Ātmikas'—Attributes—Jñāna, Dhyāna, Jīva, Tattva, and Parama.

(3) 'Vījas'—or creative potencies, such as Klim, Hlim and Slim denoting Jagannāth, Balarāma and Subhadrā and two more 'Vijas'.

At Puri, Dāmodar Svarūp enunciated the theory of 'Pañcha Tattva'.

[6]*Vaishṇava Vandana* in Sanskrit, ascribed to Jīva Gosvāmī.

[7]*Ch. Bhāgavat* III.6.473.

[8]Nityānanda along with twelve Gopālas have been mentioned in the *Jagannāth Charitāmrita*, canto—7.

Gauridās Paṇḍit was one of the closest followers of Nityānanda. Gauridās, as already stated, was the spiritual mentor of Hṛidayānanda, who was the preceptor of Balarāma Dāsa.

sound of drums and cymbals rent the air'.[9] In one of the manuscripts, ascribed to Ananta, the Master says:

> "As he (Jagannātha) speaks of the most sacred knowledge, so I give him the epithet 'very great'. Yaśovanta knows facts which are beyond comprehension of other persons. Ananta knows the science of magical symbols. Achyuta speaks of the past and present; while Balarāma expounds the principle of Yoga."

In *Chaurāśi Ājñā* we find Chaitanya seated in the Mukti Maṇḍapa of the Jagannāth temple along with five comrades, the king, and Sārvabhauma. Yaśovanta says that Chaitanya addressed each of the comrades by name to come near him. He first asked Jagannātha Dāsa.[10]

The Master declared that the five comrades were his followers in every age. He asked them to give a demonstration of their occult powers. He handed them a seed of jack fruit. The comrades caused a tree laden with jack fruits to grow from the seed. Yaśovanta heard an oracle that 'the Lord has been born at Navadvipa and is known as Chaitanya. By His command, the five comrades are born to serve Him.'[11]

Īśvara Dāsa writes that Chaitanya personally bound *Sari* (embroidered cloth) on the head of each comrade—a high honour.[12] Once he went to Cuttack from Puri to meet the comrades.[13] Chaitanya embraced each of them warmly. He discussed with them about the books they had written. Balarāma Dāsa recited from his *Rāmāyana* which was highly appreciated by the Master. Jagannātha Dāsa read some ślokas from his translation of the *Bhāgavata* which Chaitanya heard with great interest. He also held religious discourse with Jagannātha Dāsa. There was *kirtana* at Tulasipur (a part of Cuttack) which was attended by Chaitanya and the five comrades.

---

[9]*Āpaṇe Chaitanya Prabhu Sakhā bṛinda gheni*
Pañcha Sakhā mule bāra sasra Bhakta puṇi
Khola Karatālare Brahmāṇḍa uchhulai
Śūnya Saṁhitā, I.

[10]*Kahanti Chaitanya Gosāin: Pañcha Sakhānku pārśe rāi*
Boile Jagannātha Dāsa: Mora nikaṭe bege āsa
Chaurāsi Ājña—canto 42.

[11]*Janama hele Bhagavāna Chaitanya Prabhu boli jāṇa*
Tānka ajñaru Pañcha Sakhā Janma hoi saṅge lekhā,
Chaurāsi Ājñā—Ibid.

[12]*Jana Janaṅku Sāree dei Kahanti Chaitanya Gosāin,*
Chaitanya Bhāgavata—Canto 54.

[13]*Kaṭake prabeśa Chaitanya Pañchā Sakhāṅku darśana,*
Chaitanya Bhāgavata—Canto 59.

(iv) Balarama Dasa

Balarāma Dāsa was the oldest among the five comrades. He lives in the memory of the people as the author of the *Rāmāyaṇa* in Oriya. He was a Karaṇa (Kayastha) by caste.

He fought for the rights of the Śūdras (as the Non-Brahmans were generally called). In his *Vedāntasāra Gupta Gītā*, he writes that the Brahmans resented his participation in the discussion regarding Vedanta in the Mukti Maṇḍapa of the Jagannāth temple. Balarāma caused an idiot talk on Praṇava. In the *Rāmāyana*, he exposed the greedy Brahman priests of some temples which were visited by Rāma and Sītā during their exile.

Balarāma was the religious teacher of the Śūdra class. His chief seat was Gandharva maṭh on the mouth of the dead river Bānki near Puri. He was known as 'Matta' because of his madness in devotion.

We now refer to the great story teller Īśvara Dāsa. According to him, Balarāma had a vision that the Lord would incarnate again and that He would go to Nilāchala in the robes of a monk. Balarāma eagerly waited for his arrival. Chaitanya during his journey halted at Chandrapur, the native place of Balarāma, for some time. Balarāma recognized him as the Lord incarnate and forthwith he prostrated himself before his feet. 'With overflowing love, Chaitanya addressed him as Suvala and imparted the *Rāma Tāraka Parama Brahma* mantra into his ears'.[14]

Balarāma makes only one casual reference to Chaitanya in his writings (*Vedānta sāra Gupta Gitā*—XXIV) which appears to be interpolated (See footnote 4, Chapter VIII).

(v) Jagannatha Dasa

Jagannātha Dāsa's memory will be always cherished in Orissa for his translation of the *Bhāgavata Purāna*. His father was a '*Purāṇa Paṇḍa*' (reciter of the Purāṇas) in the Jagannāth temple. Jagannātha took up his father's profession. He completed the translation of the *Bhāgavata* before he met Chaitanya.[15] According to Divākara, Chaitanya gave

---

[14]*Dekhi ānanda Śrī Chaitanya* / *Suvale kale sambhāshaṇa*
Premare jara jara hoi / *Acchanti Chaitanya Gosāin*
Rāma Taraka Param Brahma / *Kahile karne Śrī Chaitanya*

Chaitanya Bhāgavata—Canto 46.

Balarāma is called Suvala also in the *Chaurāśi Ājñā*, canto—42.

[15]By translating the *Bhāgavata*, Jagannātha Dāsa incurred the displeasure of the priests who did not like that the sacred texts would be read by the common people.

The Gauḍīya Vaishṇavas take exception to his reference to Vṛindāvatī in place of Rādhā, in his translation of the *Bhāgavata*, Jagannātha writes that Vṛindāvatī was the Gopī, whom Kṛishṇa took away from the assembly of the milkmaids (*Bhāgavata*, X. 30-2). The Gauḍīya Vaishṇavas maintain that this Gopī is Rādhā herself.

Jagannātha Dāsa the epithet of '*Ati Baḍa*' for his piety and learning. But Jagannātha does not refer to Chaitanya or to other comrades in his writings. He founded the 'Ati Baḍa' sect. His chief seat is now called 'Baḍa Oriya' Maṭh. Jagannāth, the deity, communicated to Jagannātha Dāsa in a vision that at Nadiā, Chaitanya would be born as his embodiment.[16]

Jagannātha Dāsa was advised to wait under the banyan tree within the Jagannāth temple precincts. He waited for the arrival of Chaitanya with sandal paste and garlands. Seeing Chaitanya, he bowed down reverently and rubbed paste on Chaitanya's body. Then along with the five comrades, Advaita, Nityānanda, and other followers, Chaitanya visited the Jagannāth temple. He asked Jagannātha Dāsa to impart initiation to Bhānumatī, chief queen of Pratāpa Rudra.[17]

(vi) Yasovanta Dasa

Yaśovanta belongs to the Mahanāyaka or Kshatriya caste. In the *Rāsa* poems, ascribed to Yaśovanta, the amorous exploits of Rādhā and Kṛishṇa are described. Yaśovanta is chiefly remembered for his work, the *Govindachandra Tīka*, which is recited by the mendicants of the Nāth sect. He is silent about Chaitanya and other comrades in his writings. Yaśovanta, like other comrades, was a religious teacher. He established a Maṭh at Adaṅga in the Cuttack district.

Yaśovanta heard about the advent of Chaitanya. He left his home and wandered till he reached the place where Chaitanya was staying. 'He beheld the son of Śachī, who is the manifested embodiment of Jagannāth. He fell at the feet of Chaitanya and on getting up, kept his hands folded above his head.'[18] Chaitanya embraced Yaśovanta and addressed him as Suvāhu (who was Kṛishṇa's companion in the Dvāpara Yuga). Yaśovanta prayed for initiation in the name of Hari. The Master favoured him.

(vii) Achyutananda

Achyutānanda Mohanty is the patron-saint of the cowherd class. In his Maṭh at Puri a cowherd performs the daily worship. His works, the *Śūnya Saṁhitā* and the *Aṇākāra Saṁhitā* deal with the theory of Void. In the *Brahma Śāṅkuli*, the writer invokes *Alekh Purusha* or *Anādi Brahma.*

---

[16] *Chaitanya Bhāgavata* canto 45.

[17] *Chaitanya Bhāgavata* canto 46. According to the *Jagannātha Charitāmṛita*, I, Jagannātha Dāsa initiated Gaurī, the chief consort of Pratāpa Rudra.

[18] *Darśana kale Śachī suta* — *Gaurāṅga āpe Jagannāth*
Chaitanya pāda padme paḍi — *Uṭhina sire kara yoḍi*
Chaitanya Bhāgavata—Canto 46

Like Balarāma, Achyutānanda was subjected to Brahmanical persecution. They compelled him to give a demonstration of the worship of Void, in the presence of the king (see Appendix). Nembāla in the Cuttack district is the chief seat of the followers of Achyutānanda.

We will now refer to his association with Chaitanya. In the first chapter of the *Śūnya Saṁhitā* Achyutānanda writes that from his boyhood, he was devoted to Kṛishṇa. When the Master came to Puri, his father took him there. Achyutānanda writes: 'Worldly desires departed at the sight of the Master and true knowledge dawned upon his mind. The son of Śachī ordered Sanātana to impart religious instruction to Achyutānanda.'

He then returned to his native village. After some years, a great change came in his life. He heard an oracle telling him to serve Chaitanya. Forthwith he repaired to Puri and bowed at the feet of the Master. He writes: 'Out of compassion, the moon of Navadvīpa gave me cymbals and drums. . . . Kindly he taught me the tune, timing and sense of the rhythm. He taught *mantras* to me and put the cymbals into my hands.'

Achyutānanda then set out on pilgrimage and returned after some time. Thereupon he hastened to meet the Master:

> Gaurāṅgachandra, the ocean of mercy, was present on the main road. Words fail to describe the grace of the group of Vaishṇavas who thronged round him. Going in front of him, I prostrated myself at his feet and stood up. The moon of Navadvīpa was pleased at the sight of me. I received flowers and the oblation to the deity.[19]

Īśvara Dāsa as usual introduces the Lord, who delivered the following message to Achyutānanda, whom He addressed as Sudāma. Thus said the Lord 'Listen, O Achyuta to my advice. Take thy initiation from Chaitanya. Propagate the name (of Hari).' The Lord further stated 'Thou shalt serve him and follow the path of devotion. Know the *Parama Haṁsa* mantra from him. Chaitanya is identical with Me (*Chaitanya mora nija dehi*). Accept him as thy preceptor'.[20]

---

[19] *Śrī Gaurāṅgachandra karuṇā sāgara vijaye Baḍa dāṇḍare*
Vaishṇava maṛḍali beḍi sobhā tahni ki upamā debi tāre
Śrī chhamuɩe yāi śata daṇḍavata kariṇa ubhā hoili
Dekhina ānanda Navadvīpachandra prasāda phula pāili
Śūnya Saṁhitā—I

[20] *Chaitanya Bhāgavata*, canto 46 The Lord is '*Ananta murti Bhagavāna*' and '*Brahmāṇḍa Thākura*'

(viii) Ananta Dasa

Ananta Mahāpātra founded the 'Śisu' sect. His seat is at Tentuliāpaḍā in the Cuttack district. According to Īśvara Dāsa, Ananta heard an oracle that Chaitanya, the great redeemer, would repair to Nilāchala along with Nityānanda (who is the incarnation of Sankarshaṇa) and other followers. Ananta was further told that he was Dāma in the Dvāpara Yuga.

Ananta met Chaitanya, while he was resting at Konarka on his way to Puri. He fell at the feet of the Master and prayed to give him initiation. Thus said Chaitanya 'Listen, Nityānanda, my brother. Instruct Ananta in the name of Hari, which is the best thing for initiation'. Hearing this message, Nityānanda with joyful heart, imparted *mantra* to Ananta.[21]

[21] *Chaitanya prabhu ājñā hoi* *Śuna ho Nityānanda bhāi*
Ananta upadeśa kara *Harira name dikshā sāra*
Evani śuni Nityānanda *Harashe hoile ananda*
Anante upadeśa kale *karne mahāmantra dele*
Chaitanya Bhāgavata—Canto 46

APPENDIX

Difference Between the Chaitanya Faith and Orissan Vaishnavism

THIS SUBJECT matter has been discussed fully in my *History of Medieval Vaishnavism in Orissa* (pp. 147-52). Only the salient points are discussed below:

1. JAGANNATH

Medieval Vaishṇavism in Orissa centred round the worship of Jagannāth. The cult of Jagannāth was based on syncretism. Orissan Vaishṇavism absorbed many heterogeneous elements such as the Void Worship. In no other part of India there was a State deity. In the *Vata Avakāśa* attributed to Balarāma Das, Jagannāth holds a court which was attended by all other deities of Orissa. It was believed that Nīlāchala is greater than other holy places such as Mathurā, Vṛindāvana and Dvārakā (Yaśovanta Dāsa's *Prema Bhakti Brahma Gītā*, V). Divākara Dāsa writes in his *Jagannātha Charitāmṛita* (canto XVII) that Kṛishṇa is but a partial phase of Jagannāth.

According to the Gauḍīya Vaishṇavas, Jagannāth is an important Vaishṇava deity whose *darśan* during the chariot festival ensures salvation. Chaitanya indeed was deeply attached to Jagannāth whom he imagined to be Kṛishṇa at Kurukshetra. Vṛindāvana and not Nīlāchala is the chief seat of the Chaitanya faith.

2. KRISHNA

In Orissa, Kṛishṇa did not receive exclusive devotion of the Vaishṇavas before the advent of Chaitanya. To them, he was an epic god with his failings and virtues. (See Chapter X, Section III).

According to Chaitanya faith, Kṛishṇa or Bhagavat constitutes the complete manifestation of personal godhead in his perfect form. Chaitanya is believed to be the dual incarnatian of Rādhā and Kṛishṇa.

3. Radha

The *Gītā Govinda* of Jayadeva made popular in Orissa the story of Rādhā's erotic sports with Kṛishṇa. Probably in the thirteenth century, the Trinity conception (Vāsudeva, Ekānaṃśā and Sankarshaṇa) spread to Orissa. Purushottama-Jagannāth was identified with Kṛishṇa and Balarāma-Sankarshaṇa was associated with him. But Rādhā could not be accommodated in the Trinity worship in the Puri temple. Bhīma Dhivara flourished towards the end of the 15th century. In his poem '*Kapaṭa Pāśā*' he refers to Kṛishṇa, the consort of Rukminī and Satyabhāmā. According to the Chaitanya faith, Rādhā is the closest consort of Kṛishṇa and his Śakti or counterpart. Of all the Vaishṇava sects, the Chaitanya faith gives the highest place to Rādhā, next only to Kṛishṇa.

4. Mantra

The *mantra* of sixteen names and thirty two letters, consisting of 8 Hari, 4 Rāma and 4 Kṛishṇa names prevailed in Orissa even before the Chaitanya faith. The Vaishṇavas of the Orissa school adopted the *mantra* of the Vishṇusvāmī sect— 'Om Rāma Kṛishṇa Hari'. The name 'Rāma' denotes Balarāma and not the hero of the Rāmāyaṇa. In Orissan Vaishṇavism, Rāma is given precedence as the elder brother. But the Chaitanyaite Vaishṇavas recite 'Hare Krishṇa Rāma'. Kṛishṇa, being the supreme personal godhead, is superior to his brother. The Master's tongue danced while loudly reciting the Hare Krishṇa *mantra*.[22] Baladeva Vidyābhushan writes in the prologue of his commentary of the *Stavamālā* that the Hare Kṛishṇa *mantra* consists of sixteen names and thirty two letters.

According to Achyutānanda the 'Hare Rāma Kṛishṇa' *mantra* consists of thirty two letters. There were originally sixteen names out of which three were important, namely Hlim, Klim and Slim. They denoted Balarāma, Jagannāth and Subhadrā. "The Master suppressed sixteen names and introduced three names—"Hare, Rāma and Kṛishṇa."[23]

5. The Theory of Void

The Void, according to esoteric Vaishnavism, is not nothingness. The Spirit or *Purusha* immanent in Void is conceived as the Void personified. He is a transcendental entity—the total abstraction of all phenomena. But

---

[22] *Chaitanyāshtaka* I.5. in the *Stavamālā* of Rūpa Gosvāmī.

[23] *E nama gupata kari tini nāma kale*
Hare Rāma Kṛishṇa boli Prabhu ājñā dele
Śūnya Saṁhita—I

he appears in the phenomenal world in his discretion. With the growing popularity of the Kṛishṇa cult he was identified with Kṛishṇa. In Balarāma Dasa's *Virāta Gīia* I, Arjuna says to Kṛishṇa 'Thou, hast no figure or form Thou art but the Void personified' (*Śūnya Purusha Śūnya dehi*).

Achyutānanda further elaborates the theory of formless Kṛishṇa dwelling in the eternal Goloka, who is superior to Kṛishṇa of Dvārakā. Such a conception of formless Kṛishṇa is an anathema to the Chaitanya faith. · The Sahajiyā Vaishṇavas believe in supra-natural *Goloka*, where the eternal Rādhā-Kṛishṇa dally surrounded by the milkmaids.

It is stated in the *Śūnya Saṁhitā*, IX, that the eight chief consorts of Kṛishṇa at Dvārakā pressed for a glimpse of eternal Rādhā who sports with Kṛishṇa in the Rāsa arena of Goloka (eternal region). Sudāma met Kṛishṇa who blamed the consorts for their curiosity which might lead to trouble. He then sent for Garuḍa who appeared before him.

Kṛishṇa told Garuḍa to take him and the consorts to the Rāsa arena of the eternal region. Kṛishṇa however expressed his diffidence. 'How wilt thou take us to that inaccessible region?' He said: "Fear I, Kṛishṇa who is eternal" (*Mahānitya Śrī Krishnaṅku ḍarai mu puṇi*). Sudāma accompanied the party which reached as far as two 'yojanas' from the eternal region. They could not stand the glare of countless Suns and all except Sudāma retreated. Sudāma alone advanced towards the eternal region.

On the way he met one of the *Sakhīs* (female associates) who guard the region. 'Wherefrom hast thou come, my child' she asked. She explained that the eternal region has no form. Kṛishṇa is the personification of Void (*Sūnyabara boli sinā bolanti Kṛishṇaṅku*). He should be worshipped by Nirākāra *mantra* consisting of thirty-two letters. She then told that her name is Buddhamātā. Sudāma entreated her to explain the import of the Nirākārā *mantra* which she did. Buddhamātā then wended her way back to the eternal region. Sudāma returned to Dvārakā. He met Kṛishṇa and told him about his luck. Kṛishṇa observed: 'Verily hath Buddhamātā said that unalloyed devotion is derived from the worship of the formless.' He then asked Sudāma to appear in the Kali yuga to spread that knowledge. Sudama was born as Achyutananda.

6. Demonstration of the Void worship

According to the philosophy of Orissa Vaishṇavism, air can be shut out of the body by concentrating mind on some symbols, for the contemplation of the Absolute (*Parama Haṁsa*). It is stated in the *Śūnya Saṁhitā*, VII that King Pratāpa Rudra asked Achyutānanda to draw the symbols of the Void worship, before an assembly of Brahmans. Achyutānanda first sketched the diagram of Anāma (no letter) which was followed by Nāma (one letter). He then drew the symbol of Kāma Vīja (which signifies Kṛishṇa). Seeing the Sūnya *Yantra* (diagram), the Brahmans were speechless. They exclaimed 'Of a verity, you know the underlying import of the spiritual mystery'. The king said "You have indeed drawn the *yantra*. Now tell us the *mantra* and the manner in which Void is worshipped by that *mantra*.

Hearing the peremptory order of the king, Achyutānanda felt rather distressed in mind and told him that for worship of Void with *mantra* of the formless (*Mantra nirākāra Śūnya bhajana*), purification of the body and the seat would be necessary.

The Brahmans became angry at his hesitation and demanded a demonstration of the worship of Void on the spot. Achyutānanda complied with their demand. Says he "I placed the thirty two letters upon my heart and sitting straight from my navel, I became absorbed in meditation. Then with upturned face I concentrated my mind and meditated upon the formless Being. Having thus lifted life up, I was soon sitting in Void and merged myself in contemplation of *Parama Haṁsa*".

As already stated, the idea of Void worship is abhorrent to the Chaitanya faith.

CHAPTER VIII

Other Oriya Followers of Chaitanya

THE IMPORTANT Oriya followers of Chaitanya, other than the five comrades, were

(1) The followers who accepted the Chaitanya faith;
(2) The priests of the Jagannāth temple and the officers, who were ordered by the king to attend the Master; and
(3) Pratāpa Rudra, the king himself.

(1) FOLLOWERS WHO ACCEPTED THE CHAITANYA FAITH

1. *Rāmānanda*—Rāmānanda belonged to an influential karaṇa (kāyastha) family, of princely origin (*Rājavaṁsotpannajana*)[1]: Rāy was an official title. His father Bhavānanda Rāy Paṭṇaik was 'Sāmanta' (a small chief) of Bentpur near the Chilka lake. Rāmānanda was appointed the governor of the Rājya or province of Rajamahendri by Pratāpa Rudra. Rāmānanda evinced deep religious tendency. His drama, the *Jagannāth Vallabha* shows influence of the *Gītā Govinda*. He also studied the poems of Vidyāpati and composed poems in Maithili dialect.[2] His poem '*Pahilahi rāga nayana bhange bhela*' is one of the earliest poems in Maithili outside Mithilā. This poem depicting the '*Kalahantaritā*' feeling of Rādhā, is cited in the *kāvya* of Kavikarṇapūra. A portion of the poem is quoted below: "Rādhā said in a dream to the maid sent to her by her beloved Kṛishṇa, 'Love first grew into my heart from the motion of his eyes and it increased day by day and knew no bounds. And he is not my husband (Ramaṇa) nor am I his woman (*Ramaṇī*): yet love united both our souls and made us one". In this song, Rāmānanda depicts '*Prema vilāsa vivarta*' or the highest state of love, when the lover and the beloved lose

[1] *Chaitanya Chandrodaya* drama IX.

[2] A collection of poems in Bengali entitled *Daṇḍa Līlā* describes the love sports of Rādhā Kṛishṇa. The poems are attributed to Ray Rāmananda in the colophons.

their different selves and are imbued with a sense of oneness with each other. Rāmānanda's devotional poem, *Nānopachara kṛita—pujanam* has been cited in Rūpa Gosvāmī's *Padyāvalī* (No. 13). Rāmānanda's operatic play *Jagannāth-Vallabha* makes no reference to Chaitanya. It was thus written, before he met the Master.

Chaitanya during his love sickness greatly relished the description of Rādhā's *viraha* for Kṛishṇa in the *Jagannāth-Vallabha* drama.[3] The Master during the last decade of his life was overwhelmed by most distressing emotions. Rāmānanda consoled him by reciting appropriate verses from the *Gītā-Govinda* and from canto 29 of the tenth part of the *Bhāgavata.*

During his religious discourse with Chaitanya at Rājamahendri, Rāmānanda explained that '*Sahaja*' *prema* of the Gopīs is free from sensuous passion (*kāma*). This *prema* for Kṛishṇa transcends ethical barriers.[4]

Rāmānanda's greatest contribution to the doctrine of the Chaitanya faith was his delineation of 'Gopībhāva'. This idea he got from the south. In the *Chaitanya Charitāmṛita* (II.2.228) Rāmānanda tells Chaitanya that Rādhā idea is beyond comprehension. So the devotees should mentally adopt the attitude of a Gopī. (*Gopī bhāva kari aṅgikāra*).[5]

Stationed at Rajamahendri, a great centre of Telugu culture, Rāmānanda had access to South Indian devotional literature, Lilāsuka Bilvamaṅgala, author of the *Kṛishṇa Karṇāmṛita* was imbued with the feelings of a Gopī. Anḍal, a woman Ālvar poet, became inflamed with passion for Kṛishṇa and pictured herself as one of the Gopīs seeking union with Kṛishṇa, in her poem *Tiruppavai.*[6]

Rāmānanda loved pomp. While he was the governor of Rāja-mahendri he used to go ceremoniously to take bath in the Godavari. When his resignation was accepted by the king, he did not go with the Master to Puri. There would be delay he told, as 'he would be accompanied by a large retinue consisting of troops, horses and elephants.' Rāmānanda is stated to have died at Bidanasi, a suburb of Cuttack, after

---

[3]*Ch. Ch.* III.2.

Rāmānanda himself used to recite the ninth verse from the third Act of his drama, where Rādhā says to Madanikā, her companion: "The Lord knoweth not the pangs of separation."

[4]*Chaitanya Chandrodaya* VII.

[5]Ch. Ch. II.8.228. Rūpa Gosvāmī further developed the conception of *Gopī bhāva* in his poems *Chāṭupushpāñjali* and *Nāmavyuhāshṭaka.*

The devotee considers himself to be a 'Mañjarī' who finds satisfaction by serving Rādhā and Kṛishṇa during their amorous sports.

Rāmānanda discussed with Rūpa the theme of the *Vidagdha Mādhava* drama (Ch. Ch. III.2) which has a close similarity with the theme of Rāmānanda's *Jagānnāth Vallabha* drama.

[6]J.S. Hooper: *Hymns of the Alvars* p. 49 (Oxford University Press 1929).

imparting initiation to Kabīr ![7] Kṛishṇadās writes that Rāmānanda had four brothers (*Ch. Ch.* II.10). Gopīnātha was an officer in charge of a district in north Orissa. Another brother, Vāṇinātha, attended the Master. According to the *Mahabhāva Prakāśa* by Kānāi Khunṭiā, Rāmānanda had only two brothers.

2. *Mādhavi Dāsi*—Mādhavi was the foremost Vaishṇavī of the Chaitanya period in Orissa. She was a cousin of Rāmānanda and sister of Śikhi Mohanty. By virtue of her scholastic attainments, Mādhavi 'Devī' was known as the 'brother' of Śikhi Mohanty[8] She was a writer of the Temple chronicle. Madhavi was considered to be half a 'Pātra' (a favourite of Rādhā), she being a woman. In the anthology, *Padakalpataru* by Vaishṇav Dās, there are five poems of 'Mādhavi Dās' which are attributed to Mādhavī.

She could not approach Chaitanya, she being a woman. So she writes: 'Every body who beholds the face of Gorā (Gaurāṅga) floats in the stream of love. But Mādhavī has been deprived of that bliss due to her fate'. Her poem: "Jagadānanda comes from Nīlāchala to console Śachī' is bound to appeal every reader. The agony of the aged mother, whose only surviving son renounced the world, touched the heart of another old pious lady—though separated from Śachī by distance and language. In another poem she says: 'Mādhavī gave up the comfort of good garments and took the dress of an anchoress'[9].

3. *Balarāma*—Vṛindāvan Dās refers to a 'Matta' Balarāma Dāsa. Probably, he is one of the five comrades. Another Balarāma was the son of Kānāi Khunṭia.

4. *Gapāla Guru*—Gopāla was the son of Murāri Kar. From his boyhood he served the Master in the house of Kāśī Miśra. Chaitanya gave him this name and put him in charge of the Kṛishṇa image, which was worshipped in the house of Kāśī Miśra, by putting 'Ṭikā' or mark of sandal paste on his forehead.[10]. The house of Kāśī Miśra is now known as the Rādhākānta Maṭh. Gopāla took initiation from Vakreśvar Puṇḍit.

5. *Jagannātha*—Devaki Nandan writes that he was a great singer whose songs pleased Jagannāth. He may be identified with '*Ati Baḍa*' Jagannāth Dāsa. One Jagannātha Mohanty dressed as Yaśodā during the Nandotsava festival in 1512.

---

[7] *Chaitanya Bhāgavata*, canto 65.
[8] Kāvya of Kavikarṇapūra, XIII.90.
[9] *Padakalpataru* No. 1786.
[10] *Vaishnava Vandanā* by Devaki Nandan.

6. *Kānāi (Kanhei) Khunṭia*—The work of Khunṭiā was to supply garlands to Jagannāth. The Nandotsava festival, which follows Kṛishṇa's birth day, was solemnly held in 1512, after the Master's return from the south. Kānāi took the role of Nanda. Chaitanya acted as Kṛishṇa and bowed down to him.[11] Kānāi wrote a poem in Bengali. The ending couplet is cited below: "Says Kānāi Khunṭia. It seems to my mind that the flute kills only the helpless women"[12] He wrote also the *Mahābhāva Prakāśa* in Oriya.

7. *Kāśī (śvara) Miśra*—He was in charge of the affairs of the Jagannāth temple. Chaitanya resided in one of the inside rooms in his house as it was situated near the Jagannāth temple.[13] In the poem *Stavakalpataru*, Raghunāth Dās Gosvāmī has described the ecstatic emotions of Chaitanya in the *āvāsa* (house) of Kāśīśvara Miśra. He has been highly praised for his piety in the *Vaishṇava Vandanā* in Sanskrit, ascribed to Jīva Gosvāmī.

8. *Mādhava Patnaik*—His name has been mentioned in *Vaishṇava Vandanā* works of Vrindāvan Dās II, Devaki Nandan and of Jīva Gosvāmī. He was probably related to Rāmānanda.

9. *Māmu Thākur*—He was a priest of the Gopināth temple. According to the *Bhakti Ratnakār*, Chaitanya passed away in the temple of Gopināth in his presence.

10. *Paramānanda Mahapātra*—Paramānanda was an attendant of the Jagannāth temple. Vṛindāvan Dās praises his devotion to Chaitanya.[14]

11. *Pradumnya Miśra*—Sārvabhauma introduced him to Chaitanya[15]. He was advised by Chaitanya to take religious instruction from Rāmānanda.

12. *Śankar Paṇḍit*—He and his brother Dāmodar were devoted to Chaitanya.[16]

13. *Śikhi Mohanty*—He was a scribe of the Jagannāth temple. Śikhi was a 'Pātra' like his sister Mādhavi, Rāmānanda and Svarūp Dāmodar.[17]

---

[11] *Ch. Ch.* II.15.
[12] *Aprakāsita Padaratnāvali* No. 414.
[13] *Ch. Chandrodaya* VIII.5.
[14] *Ch. Bhāgavat* III.4.
[15] *Ch. Chandrodaya* VIII.2.
[16] *Ch. Bhāgavat* III.3.
[17] *Ch. Ch.* III.2.

His brother Murāri also was a devotee. Murāri followed his brother's profession.

14. *Svāpneśvara*—This Brahman invited Chaitanya to be his guest at Cuttack.[18]

15. *Tulasi Miśra*—He was a high priest (*Parichhā*) of the Jagannāth temple. He participated in the Nandotsava festival in 1512 along with Kāśī Miśra and king Pratāpa Rudra.

The names of a few more Oriya followers of Chaitanya are known from the *Vaishṇava Vandanā* works. Rāmachandra, Raghunāth, and Śivānanda Paṇḍit were Brahmans. Vipradāsa, Baladeva Mohanty, Kāśīnāth Mohanty and Vishṇudāsa were non-Brahmans.

II The Priests and the Officials

The second group consists of the Jagannāth temple priests and some officers of the king. They honoured the Master as a great saint and as a very consequential person, being highly respected by the king himself. When the Master expressed his desire to clean the Guṇḍichā temple, the Temple *Parichhā* (Superintendent) replied: 'We are all your servants bound to do whatever you wish for. On me has been laid the special command of the king to quickly perform whatever you wish.'[19]

Jagannath Temple Priests

Janārdana dressed the body of Jagannāth. Simheśvara and Murāri conducted the worship of Jagannāth. Kṛishṇadāsa held the golden rod of Jagannāth. The names of the priests Praharāja Mahāpātra and Dāsa Mahasupakāra (the kitchen superintendent) are not known. Two royal officers are known only from their surnames Maṅgrāj and Harichandan. They were deputed by the king to attend Chaitanya during his journey to Bengal.

III Pratapa Rudra

It is stated in the Sanskrit and Bengali biographies of Chaitanya that Pratāpa Rudra was converted to the Chaitanya faith. The king handed over his kingdom to his son, in order to spend his time in the company of the Master.[20] Vṛindāvan Dās gives an embellished account of Pratāpa

[18] *Ch. Ch.* II.16.
[19] *Ch. Ch.* II.12.75.
[20] Narahari Chakravarti: *Bhakti Ratnākar*, III. p. 111.

Rudra's devotion to Chaitanya. He writes that the king did not like Chaitanya's appearance, smeared with saliva and dust, during *kirtana* before the chariot of Jagannāth. At night, the king saw Jagannāth in a dream, smeared with saliva and dirt. He also saw Chaitanya seated on the throne of Jagannāth. The king bitterly repented for his mistake. He went to the flower garden, where Chaitanya was seated along with his followers, and fell at his feet. The Master blessed him and said "Let your mind be devoted to Kṛishṇa. Do nothing else but the work of Kṛishṇa. Chant always the name of Kṛishṇa".[21] Act VIII of the *Chaitanya Chandrodaya* drama is named '*Pratapā Rudra anugraha*'.

Even after his contact with Chaitanya, the king did not permanently stay at his palace at Puri. He used to attend the festivals of Jagannāth. During the chariot festivals he came to Puri to sweep the cars of the deities. He certainly met Chaitanya whenever he came to Puri. Religiously minded, Pratāpa Rudra was impressed when he witnessed the spiritual ecstasy of the Master. The king ordered the Jagannāth temple priests to carry out the wishes of the Master. He also ordered the royal officers to arrange accommodation for Chaitanya and his party during his journey to Bengal and 'to wait on him day and night'. He also participated in the Nandotsava festivals in which Chaitanya took part.

All these facts do not prove that he accepted the Chaitanya faith. Pratāpa Rudra was well-read in Kṛishṇaite theology. He quoted appropriate verses from the *Bhāgavata*, when he first met Chaitanya, which were appreciated by the Master. Pratāpa Rudra's court-poet Jīvadeva wrote the *Bhakti Baibhava kāvya*, expounding the esoteric principles of devotion, for which the king honoured him with the presentation of a drum (ḍiṇḍima).

Pratāpa Rudra continued to evince interest in the esoteric Vaishṇava philosophy which was advocated by five contemporary religious teachers, who were known as the five comrades. Balarāma Dāsa writes in his *Vata Avakāśa* that some missing ornaments of Jagannāth were returned by him. The king scolded him for stealing Jagannāth's ornaments. Balarāma told him that Jagannāth came to his Maṭh and left the ornaments in his custody. The king praised him for devotion.

It is stated in the *Vedāntasāra Gupta Gitā*, XXIX, that the Brahmans complained against Balarāma Dāsa for participating in the discussion of Vedānta within the Jagannāth temple. The king sided with them. Balarāma made an idiot talk on Vedanta. It is said that king Pratāpa Rudra exclaimed: 'Chaitanya indeed is my preceptor. But you are a greater preceptor to me'.[22]

---

[21] *Ch. Bhāgavat* III.5.

[22] These lines in the Union Press publication of the *Vedāntasara Gupta Gītā* (XXIV), are not to be found in the Utkal Sahitya Press publication of that book.

In the *Amarakosha Gītā*, Balarāma Dāsa praises Pratāpa Rudra for his devotion to the Vaishṇavas (canto-7). Achyutānanda gave a demonstration of the worship of Void by controlling air within the body. The king was pleased. He praised him unreservedly and gave away land to build a Maṭh on the sea coast. Achyutānanda was a boy when he first met Chaitanya. He gave the demonstration after some years. Thus Pratāpa Rudra was interested in the demonstration of the Void worship even after his close contact with Chaitanya.

Jagannātha Dāsa, like other comrades, enjoyed the patronage of the king. He imparted *mantra* to the chief queen of Pratāpa Rudra. The king gave him land where the Maṭh of the Atibaḍi sect of Jagannātha Dāsa is now located.

Yaśovanta Dasa did not lag behind his friends in the demonstration of occult powers. Thus, when he became famous as a religious teacher, Pratāpa Rudra sent for him. He astonished the king by causing leaves to grow on a dead tree.[23]

Pratāpa Rudra was eclectic in his religious outlook. He worshipped Heramba (Gaṇesa) for good fortune.[24] Durgā has been propitiated in the same inscription by land grant, for meeting the expenses of worship in her temple. In the beginning of his law digest entitled *Sarasvatī Vilāsam*, Pratāpa Rudra calls himself 'Śrī Durgā Baraputra'.

It appears that the contact between the king and Chaitanya became less frequent during the last years of Chaitanya, when he suffered from love sickness. As S.K. De has remarked: "As a man of devout inclinations, he (Pratāpa Rudra) was probably impressed by the religious personality of Chaitanya and paid a willing homage, but beyond this, there is no evidence of Pratāpa Rudra's actual conversion."[25]

---

[23]*Chaurāsi Ājñā* canto 39.

[24]The Velicherla inscription A.R. 12 of 1920-21.

[25]De: Op. cit. p. 90 fn.

CHAPTER IX

Chaitanya's Influence on History of Orissa

I—POLITICAL CONDITION

R.D. BANERJEE in his *History of Orissa* (Vol. I, pp 330-2) had created the impression that the Chaitanya faith (which is called Neo-Vaishṇavism by Banerjee) was mainly responsible for the fall of the empire of Crissa.[1]

This question has been fully discussed in my book *History of the Gajapati Kings of Orissa* pp. 102-7. I shall refer only to the sal ent points raised by Banerjee. He writes:

> Suddenly from the beginning of the 16th century, a decl ne set in the power and prestige of Orissa with the corresponding decline in the military spirit of the people. The decline is intimately connected with the long residence of the Bengali Vaishṇava saint Chaitanya in the country. If we accept one-tenth of what the Bengali and Sanskrit biographies of the saint state about his influence over Pratāpa Rudra and the people of the country, we must admit that Chaitanya was one of the principal causes of the political decline of the empire and the people of Orissa.

The Sanskrit and Bengali biographies, however, nowhere state that the king gave up his royal duties and stayed at Puri. R.D. Banerjee has deliberately mis-stated facts to prove Chaitanya's responsibility for the fall of Orissa. His acceptance of only 'one-tenth' is a skilful attempt to create impression. Banerjee refers to the 'great hold' which Chaitanya came to possess over Pratāpa Rudra and consequently, 'the decline in the military

[1]D.R. Banerjce wrote the *History of Orissa* with the patronage of the then Mahārāja of Mayurbhanj. One of the main causes of the spread of the Chaitanya f ith in Orissa was its acceptance by the Mahārājas of Mayurbhanj, who headed the prir cely rulers of the Orissan States.

spirit of the people'. Even after meeting Chaitanya in 1512, Pratāpa Rudra did not give up warfare. In 1514, he marched southward to raise the siege of Udayagiri by Kṛishṇadeva Rāya. In January 1516 he marched again to save Koṇḍapalli 'but he was defeated and put to flight' (Nuniz).

It may be argued that Pratāpa Rudra lost military vigour due to his contact with Chaitanya, which led to his defeat at the hands of Kṛishṇadeva Rāya. But Pratāpa Rudra's defeat was partly due to the almost simultaneous attacks from two frontiers. In 1509, he had gone to the south, in view of the hostile preparations of Kṛishṇadeva Rāya. The invasion of Husain Shah in 1511 compelled him to march up to the northern frontier of Orissa to expel the enemy. He again went back as far south as the banks of the Nellore river to guard his southern frontier. In 1512 he returned to his capital. These journeys exhausted his army. Thus Husain Shah's raid into Northern Orissa indirectly helped Kṛishṇadeva Rāya to gain a decisive victory over Pratāpa Rudra.

At the same time it must be admitted that the king of Vijayanagar was an able commander and his well-planned Orissa campaigns which began in 1513 give an indication of his brilliant and forceful personality. Thus he could easily out-general his adversary, a man of peaceful disposition.

Pratāpa Rudra must be blamed for neglecting the defences of the military outposts in the Godāvari-Kṛishṇā Doab. Quli-Qutb Shah of Golkoṇḍa encountered little resistance when he seized Koṇḍapalli, probably in 1531. The whole of the Kṛishṇā-Godāvarī Doab was lost to Orissa shortly after the death of Pratāpa Rudra. The sense of frustration caused by the humiliating peace with Kṛishṇadeva Rāya and the suicide of his only competent son Vīrabhadra under tragic circumstances made a deep impression upon Pratāpa Rudra's mind. He eschewed militarism for which Chaitanya can hardly be blamed. In spite of his religiosity which now became more pronounced, Pratāpa Rudra left his successors an extent of territory which was held by the Gaṅga kings in their palmy days.

Some more fallacious arguments of R.D. Banerjee are:

(1) 'The acceptance of Vaishṇavism rather Neo-Vaishṇavism was the real cause of the Muslim conquest of Orissa twentyeight years after the death of Pratāpa Rudra'. The Chaitanya faith hardly made any substantial progress in Orissa during the life time of Chaitanya. The real cause of the fall of Orissa was not the acceptance of Neo-Vaishṇavism but the weakness of Pratāpa Rudra's successors and treachery of the officers. Pratāpa Rudra died in 1540 and within 28 years, no less than seven kings of three different dynasties occupied the throne. It is difficult to link the sickening tale of moral turpitude with the Chaitanya faith in Orissa—which taught mankind to be honest.

The story of the conquest of West Bengal by Bakhtiyar Khalji is a disgraceful one and no devotion to a religious movement serves as an extenuating cause in that case. Had there been no Chaitanya movement, even then the succession of the weaklings, the moral degeneration of the high officials of the State and the decline in the military strength of the nation after the crushing defeat at the hands of Kṛishṇadeva Rāya—would have brought about the downfall of Orissa, sooner or later.

(2) Banerjee points out that according to Jayānanda's *Chaitanya Maṅgal*, Chaitanya dissuaded Pratāpa Rudra from invading Bengal because the war would have a disastrous effect on his country. Banerjee remarks that 'the advice of Chaitanya was sufficient to cause this cowardly and religiously minded king to desist from a proper defence of his own territories' (by retaliating Husain Shah's invasion).

Banerjee depended on the eight lines of the chapter 'Vijay Khaṇḍa' quoted in the introduction (p. 6) of the printed text of *Chaitanya Maṅgal* edited by N.N. Vasu. But these lines have not been inserted in 'Vijay Khaṇḍa' (pp. 139-45). Dr. B.B. Majumdar suggests that N.N. Vasu had doubt regarding the genuineness of these lines.[2]

Even assuming that these lines were genuine and not interpolated Jayānanda's statement is not tenable. In 1512, the king came to Puri to participate in the Car festival. Kṛishṇadās Kavirāj writes that the king expressed his desire before Sārvabhauma to meet Chaitanya. Said Sārvabhauma to the Master: 'Here is Pratāpa Rudra, eager to meet you'. The Master clasped his hands to his ears, murmured an appeal to God, and replied 'why such an improper speech, Sārvabhauma? For me, to meet a king or a woman is fatal like a drought of poison.'[3]

It is hardly believable that in spite of his categorical denial to meet Pratāpa Rudra as a king, Chaitanya gave him advice on matters of war and external policy.

The inscriptional evidence also goes against the assumption that Chaitanya was the political adviser to the king. Jayānanda writes that 'Chaitanya advised the king to conquer Kāñchīdeśa instead of Bengal'. The king acted accordingly and proceeded southward to fight with Vijayanagar. In 1513 and in 1516, Pratāpa Rudra marched to the south, not to conquer the province of Chandragiri in which Kānchī was situated, but to defend his own territory which was attacked by Kṛishṇadeva Rāya. Thus the statement of Jayānanda must be rejected.

(3) Banerjee points out that Gopīnātha Patnaik, brother of Rāmā-

---

[2]C.C.U. p. 248.

[3]*Chaitanya Chandrodaya*, VIII: Ch. Ch. II.11.

nanda, embezzled public money and was ordered by the king to be put to death. But Gopīnātha was saved and reinstated at the intervention of Chaitanya's disciples. It is indeed difficult to exonerate the conduct of these disciples who intervened to save Gopīnātha's life after Chaitanya's flat refusal to do so. But it was natural that influence was exerted to save from painful execution the brother of Rāy Rāmānanda, a punishment surely out of proportion for a crime likc embezzlement.

(4) Banerjee feelingly speaks of Rāmānanda's betrayal of the interests of his own people "by retiring from his position from the weakest frontier of his country". This involves the supposition that Rāmānanda was a capable officer, whose retirement spelt ruin to his country. According to him 'Rāmānanda governed to the southern viceroyalty'. Banerjee's statements show his ignorance regarding the contemporary history of Orissa. There were three Rājyas or provinces in the south of Orissa. Rāmānanda was the Governor of the northernmost Rājya of Rājamahendri. Banerjee conveniently forgets that the weakest frontier of Orissa was in the north—through which the Muslims constantly made aggressive inroads and finally destroyed the independence of the country. Rāmānanda, a theologically-minded scholar, proved a failure as an administrator and did well by resigning his post, for which he was unfit by temperament. The Gajapati king himself complained that Rāmānanda did not properly maintain the revenue accounts[4] but did not take any action.

We reiterate the fact that the Chaitanya faith did not spread in Orissa during the life time of Chaitanya. Oblivious of all political affairs, the Master constantly chanted the name of Kṛishṇa. Religious-minded officers like Rāmānanda retired from service and joined him while his brother Gopīnātha was not chastened by the teachings of Chaitanya.

The Chaitanya faith had no effect on Govinda Vidyādhara and Mukunda Harichandan who murdered the sons of their masters to ascend the throne; Narasiṁha Jena the parricide king; Raghu Bhañja Chhotarai, Rāmachandra Bhañja, Śikhi and Mānāi Mahāpātra—the traitors; and on Dānpahantā Singh who betrayed the location of Jagannāth to Kālā Pāhāḍ in 1568.

II—SOCIETY

Chaitanya's influence on the socio-religious life of Orissa has been criticized by M. Mansinha in his book, *History of Oriya Literature*. He

[4] *Ch. Ch.* III.9.

writes: 'The Brahmins are as a class intensely hostile to Chaitanyaism and some of its ceremonies even today'. In the writings of some of them "we find a bitter diatribe against the Chaitanyaian Bhakti cult and its evil effect on Orissa's social life". Mansinha remarks: "It is typical of the general attitude of the Orissa intelligentsia" (p. 89). Vague criticism utilises emotion and not facts. Many Brahmans in Orissa are hostile to the Chaitanyaian Bhakti cult because it makes no discrimination between the Brahmans and the non-Brahmans.

Mansinha next attacks the Rādhā-Kṛishṇa cult. He writes: "As against the Radha-Krishna cult which Chaitanya universalised in Orissa, thus doing eternal harm to the nation's character training and social morals, the book of Jagannatha Dasa (*the Bhagavata*) has laid what foundation there is in the Oriyas, of healthy piety and morality"*.

The Kṛishṇa cult prevailed in Orissa even before the advent of Chaitanya. Mārkaṇḍa Dāsa wrote the *Keśava Koili* in the 15th century. Jagannātha Dāsa translated the *Bhāgavata* before he met Chaitanya. In the tenth part of the work, which is popular in Orissa, Kṛishṇa's erotic sport with the Gopīs has been described. Achyutānanda translated the *Harivaṁsa*, narrating the life story of Kṛishṇa. The *Gītā-Govinda* made the Rādhā-Kṛishṇa theme popular, when the literary revival took place in the fifteenth century.

Rāmānanda, in his *Jagannath-Vallabha* drama describes the dalliance of Rādhā and Kṛishṇa. In Orissa, the Rādhā-Kṛishṇa cult received impetus during the Chaitanya period. But it was universally accepted by the masses, when Śyāmānanda and other Vaishṇava teachers spread the Chaitanya faith in Orissa in the seventeenth century.

III—RELIGION

Chaitanya did not preach any faith in Orissa nor did he initiate any person. Nevertheless, his influence on the religious history of Orissa was profound. Before the advent of Chaitanya, Kṛishṇa did not occupy a high place in popular imagination. He was criticized by Sāralā Dāsa in the *Mahabhārata* (*Mushali Parva*) for immorality.[5] Chaitanya Dāsa vilified Kṛishṇa in the *Nirguṇa Saṁhitā*, XVI. Chaitanya's teachings brought about a radical change in the conception and the Rādhā-Kṛishṇa cult was exalted by the contemporary writers.

---

[5]"The poet has depicted Kṛishṇa in many places as an insincere self-applauding person revelling in vile plans."

Mrityunjay Rath—*Sāralā Charitā* p. 84.

*p. 99. The traitors mentioned in Section I of this chapter did nor read the book of Jagannatha Dasa.

The five comrades wrote poems on *Rāsa* or the sport of Kṛishṇa with Rādhā and the Gopīs. Jagannātha Dāsa wrote a poem, the *Rāsa-kriḍā*. Achyutānanda described eternal *Rāsa* in the region of Void in his work, the *Nitya Rāsa*. In the *Śūnya Saṁhita*, X, mundane Kṛishṇa and his consorts unsuccessfully tried to reach the eternal *Rāsa* arena. In the *Prema Bhakti Brahma Gitā*, Yaśovanta Dāsa praises the mode of devotion through *Gopī Bhāva*.[6] In Ananta Dasa's *Thula Śūnya Rāsa*, Rādhā explains the principles of *yoga*. Chaitanya made popular the conception of identity of Jagannāth with Kṛishṇa.[7] During the 'Herā Pañchamī' festival, it is believed that Jagannāth-Kṛishṇa longs for Vṛindāvana. "If the rites of Jagannāth are analysed, it will be seen that he has become to a great extent Gauḍīya Vaishṇava".[8]

Another contribution of Chaitanya was the *Nagara kiratna* in which all persons, irrespective of their sectarian beliefs, can participate. But the greatest contribution of Chaitanya to the religious history of Orissa was his imagery (*Bhāvamūrti*). A great apostle possessing divine personality lived at Puri for twenty years. 'In Chaitanya' writes A.K. Majumdar 'religious devotion saw its extreme limits of rapturous expression, both physically and psychologically, which is perhaps unparallelled in the history of religion".[9] Even Mansinha admits: 'To the masses of Orissa, he proved to be a veritable fountainhead of unprecedented spiritual enthusiasm. Even today, to the millions of Orissa, Chaitanya is the only God'.[10]

While referring to Chaitanya's influence upon the masses in Orissa, we should not ignore the fact that the Chaitanya faith did not spread throughout Orissa. It is popular only in the coastal districts of Balasore, Cuttack, Puri, Ganjam and in the adjoining districts of Keonjhar Mayur-

---

[6] "Fortunate are those who serve (mentally) the milkmaids".
Prema Bhakti Brahma Gitā—III.

[7] Surendra Mohanty: *Oriya Sāhityara madhya parva* p. 92.
Jagannāth is worshipped also by the mantra "*Klim Krishṇāya Govindāya Gopījanaballabhāya namah*".
K.C. Misra: *The Cult of Jagannāth* p. 144.

[8] N. Samantaraya—*Oḍiyā Vaishṇava Sāhitya* p. 3.
The faces of the tower of the Jagannāth temple are carved with the figures of Kṛishṇa with two cowherd boys and with the scene of Kṛishṇa killing the Kāliya serpent.

[9] A.K. Majumdar—*Chaitanya: His Life and Doctrine* p. 269.

[10] M. Mansinha—*History of Oriya literature* p. 90.
Kennedy expresses a similar opinion: "Orissa became such a stronghold of the Chaitanya faith that today the name of Gauranga is more commonly reverenced in Orissa than in Bengal itself."
Kennedy: The *Chaitanya Movement* p. 75.

bhanj, Dhenkanal and Korapat.[11]

In coastal Orissa, most of the Brahmans were opposed to Chaitanya-ism, though some of them took the Vaishṇava surname 'Dās'. Chaitanya came to Orissa at a time when the non-Brahmans challenged the monopoly of the Brahmans in intellectual pursuits. Rāmānanda, the most prominent follower of Chaitanya in Orissa was a non-Brahman. Two non-Brahmans, Śyāmānanda and Rasika Murāri, spread the Chaitanya faith in Orissa in the seventeenth century. Baladeva Vidyabhushan, another non-Brahman, was the greatest exponent of the dogmas of the faith in the eighteenth century. The Oriya Brahmans did not like the Chaitanya movement, dominated by the 'Śūdras'.

More than a century ago, Hunter wrote:

> The adoration of Chaitanya has become a sort of family worship throughout Orissa.———The worship of Chaitanya extends throughout Orissa and I have a long list of landed families who worship him with daily rituals in household chapels, dedicated to his name. At this moment, Chaitanya is the apostle of the common people in Orissa. The Brahmans, unless they happen to enjoy grants of lands in his name, ignore his work. In almost every Brahman village, the communal shrine is dedicated to Śiva, but in the villages of ordinary husbandmen, it is Vishṇu who is worshipped and Chaitanya is remembered as the great teacher of the proletarian faith.[12]

It will be wrong to ignore the adverse effects of the Chaitanya faith on the cultural heritage of Orissa. The theories of the Void worship, formless Kṛishṇa and of Buddha-Jagannāth are considered heretical by the Oriya Vaishṇavas professing the Chaitanya faith.

The mediums of *kirtana,* called the *Nadiā kirtana* are Oriya and Bengali. Some years ago, the present writer spent a night in a village the inhabitants of which had no knowledge of the Bengali language. But early in the morning some of them sang *Prem bilāte nagara pathe Nitai*

---

[11]West Orissa was separated by dense forests and had little contact with north-eastern Orissa (subsequently known as Katak Subah) till the Maratha rule in Orissa. The chiefs of West Orissa continued allegiance to their tutelary goddesses. The zamindars of Ganjam and of Jeypore accepted the Chaitanya faith and their subjects followed their examples.

[12]*Orissa* Vol. I p. 109. In the Balasore district, Chaitanya is worshipped by the cultivator caste. In each village there is an 'Adhikāri' or non-Brahman priest to conduct the worship. Some scheduled castes in north Orissa profess Vaishṇavism. In the Balasore and Cuttack districts, many of the Kaṇḍrās and Pānos—worship Rādhā, Kṛishṇa, and Chaitanya. Such Kaṇḍrās in the Balasore district are called Kālandi Vaishṇavas.

Gaur elore (Nityānanda and Gaurāṅga have come to the street to spread the devotional love). Ignorance of the language was no bar to the sincerity of their devotion.

The Chaitanya faith in Orissa assimilated the cult of Jagannāth. According to Īśvara Dāsa, Jagannāth swallowed Chaitanya. Chaitanyaism in Orissa swallowed Jagannāthism.

CHAPTER X

Vaishnavism in Orissa in the 16th Century

I—JAGANNĀTH

THE INFLUENCE of Jagannāth reached its zenith during the 100 years 1467-1567. Kapilendra died on the banks of the Krishna in 1467. Before his death he proclaimed his younger son Purushottama as his successor, believing that Jagannāth had urged him to do so in a dream.[1]

It is almost certain that popular belief in the dispensation of Jagannāth in Purushottama's favour enabled Purushottama to gain the throne, disinheriting his elder brother Hamvīra, who had a more brilliant military career than Purushottama. The king-maker Jagannāth also prominently figures in the Kāñchī-Kāverī tradition according to which Jagannāth and Balarāma took part in war in the guise of horsemen and helped Purushottama to gain Kāñchī and the hands of the Kāñchī princess.

The first inscription of Pratāpa Rudra who came to the throne in 1497, records his devotion for Jagannāth. Such was the prestige and glory of Jagannāth when Chaitanaya first came to Puri in April 1510. The prevailing form of Vaishṇavism at that time may be called as the Jagannāth cult. Different sects of Vaishṇavism existed in Orissa under the aegis of Jagannāth-Vishṇu.[2] In 1511 the Muslim raid was hurried and the damage to the Jagannath temple was not extensive. Jagannāth came back to his temple from his hiding place on the Chilka coast. His festivals were conducted with great enthusiasm, as evident from Kṛishṇa-

[1]A.R. Inscription No. 226 of 1935-36 refers to Purushottama Gajapati, who was blessed by Jagannāth (*Jagannāth vara prasāda*).

[2]There were Maṭhs of the Śrī, Nimbārka and Vishṇusvāmi sects at Puri in the sixteenth century. 'They shed their angularities—gathering under the shadow of Jagannāth'. (Sir Jadunath Sarkar in the preface of my book, *History of Medieval Vaishnavism in Orissa*). It is curious that the Gauḍīya and Oriya biographers of Chaitanya are silent about Chaitanya's contact with other Vaishṇava sects at Puri.

dās Kavirāj's descriptions of the chariot festivals. Jagannāth, was at the height of his splendour, before the eclipse took place.

The five comrades wrote poems in adoration of Jagannāth. Balarāma Dāsa named his translation of the Sanskrit *Rāmāyana, Jagmohan Rāmāyana* in honour of the deity. In the first part of the work, Jagannāth—Kṛishṇa has been exalted as king with Rukmiṇī his consort as queen. In the Vata Avakāsa, Balarāma Dāsa accompanies Jagannāth to Lankā. Lakshmī within the Jagannāth temple precincts, is the object of adoration in Balarāma's *Lakshmī Purāṇa.* In Balarāma's *Vedāntasara Gupta Gītā* and in Achyutānanda's *Śūnya Purāna*, I, Jagannath has been described as the embodiment of all the incarnations of vishṇu. In the third canto of the *Prema Bhakti Brahma Gītā*, Krishna says that all *Tīrthas* (holy places) are concentrated in Nīlāchala, which is far superior to Dvārakā, Mathurā and Vṛindāvana. Jagannātha Dāsa is said to be the author of the *Daru Bramha Gītā*, which describes the transformation of Kṛishṇa's body into sacred Log.

Chaitanya probably passed away in the temple of Jagannath. That melancholy event did not stop the month long celebration of the *Chandan yātrā* (*Śūnyā Saṁhitā, I*). The temple services were conducted as usual, though the temple was no longer visited by the greatest devotee of Jagannāth. Pratāpa Rudra came every year to participate in the festivals. Rāmānanda, Kāśi Misra, Jagannātha Dāsa and other Oriya companions of Chaitanya as usual visited the temple. They must have missed keenly the tall and lustrous figure of the Master, blissfully gazing at Jagannāth from the Garuḍa pillar.

After some years Pratāpa Rudra died. Govinda Vidyādhar who seized the throne after murdering the sons of Pratāpa Rudra also professed devotion to Jagannāth. In his inscription in the Jagannāth temple, he threatened the feudatory chiefs with displeasure of Jagannāth if they rebel against him. In 1568 Kālā Pāhād, general of the Sultan of Bengāl'. invaded Orissa. Mukundadeva, the last Hindu king of Orissa, was defeated and killed. Kālā Pāhād made a surprise raid on the Jagannāth temple. On the approach of Kālā Pāhād, the image of Jagannāth was taken out of the temple and removed to a secret place. Unfortunately, the location of the image was betrayed to the iconoclast. "Kālā Pāhād flung the idol into fire and burnt it and afterwards cast it into the sea.[3]

Besara Mohanty, a mendicant, procured the ashes of the burnt image and went to Khurdā. The Raja of Khurdā constructed a Jagannāth temple at Khurdā. It is stated in the *Mādāla Pāñjī*, the Jagannāth temple chronicle, (which was written under the patronage of the Khurdā Raja's) that Rāmachandra Deva, Raja of Khurdā, installed

[3]Abul Fazl: *Ain-i-Akbari* (Eng trans) Vol. II p. 128

a new image of Jagannāth in the Puri temple in 1575, with much pomp and splendour. It is difficult to believe that the fanatic Afghans allowed the worship of Jagannāth at Puri within seven years after the destruction of the image. Till more definite evidence is available, it is safer to assume that the temple of Jagannāth was empty from 1568 to 1589.

In 1589, Raja Mānsingh defeated the Afghans. According to the terms of the treaty the temple of Jagannāth and its surrounding areas were made crown land. It appears that an image of Jagannāth was installed after this treaty in the Puri temple. But 'the wicked Afghans laid hold of the temple of worship of Jagannāth'.[4] Probably the temple was again desecrated. Raja Mānsingh conquered Orissa for the second time. The Raja of Khurda was made the custodian of the temple. But the glory of the temple could not be restored.

Throughout the reign of Jahangir, Jagannāth passed through bad days. His temple became a target of attack by the Subadars of Orissa. Keshodās Maru, a Rajput Officer in the Mughal army, forcibly occupied the temple. He plundered the temple property and scourged the Brahmans to disgorge more property.[5]

The desecration of the Jagannāth temple, the destruction of the image of Jagannāth and his absence from his temple for 21 years, tarnished the fame of Jagannāth. The conception of his infallibility was gone.[6] He was no longer the State deity, served by the mighty rulers of a large kingdom. The temple was plundered and the priests were beaten even by a Hindu.

The collapse of the prestige of Jagannāthism indirectly contributed to the spread of Chaitanyaism. Broken in spirit, the people now sought solace in the Rādhā-Kṛishṇa cult, as preached by the Oriya spiritual teachers of the Chaitanya faith.

II—PROMINENT GAUDIYA FOLLOWERS

The sudden passing away of the Master was a great blow to his faith. Puri lost its importance as the chief seat of the sect. The rulers after Pratāpa Rudra evinced little interest in the promotion of the Chaitanya faith. They cared more for palace intrigues than for salvation. Nonetheless, the Chaitanya faith gradually spread in Orissa. Six Gauḍīya

---

[4] Abul Fazl: *Akbarnama* (Eng trans) Vol. III p. 934

[5] Mirza Nathan: *Bahāristān-i-Gaibī* (Eng trans) pt 1 p. 35

[6] The wives of the priests of the Jagannāth temple took shelter in the temple. They did not believe that the Muslims would pull down the shrine. They said "Oh! how could it occur ? And how could they have power to hurt the deity ?" Niamat-ulah's *Makhzan-i-Afghāna* quoted in the *Bengal Past and Present* Vol. 72 p. 22

followers of Chaitanya are connected with the Chaitanya faith in Orissa. Svarūp Dāmodar was one of them. He propounded the doctrine of 'Pañcha Tattva' or five great persons. The Oriya Vaishṇavas invoke 'Pañcha Tattva' on special occasions.

(i) Svarup Damodar

Svarūp Dāmodar was a Brahman of Navadvīpa. He was attached to Chaitanya from his boyhood. He also became a monk when Chaitanya took initiation as an ascetic and settled at Puri. Svarūp Dāmodar and Rāmānanda were the closest companions of Chaitanya. Svarūp Dāmodar constantly attended the Master during the years of love sickness. He was highly respected by the Gauḍiya Vaishṇavas.

To Svarūp Dāmodar goes the credit of preventing schism in the Chaitanya sect. After the passing away of Chaitanya, his faith underwent rapid change. '*Guruvāda*' prevailed in Neo-Chaitanyaism. Nityānanda, Advaita, Gadādhar and Narahari Sarkar had a large number of disciples who criticized each other.[7] To reconcile the divergent groups Svarūp Dāmodar named Chaitanya and four of his Brahman associates, Advaita, Nityānanda, Srivās, and Gadādhar Paṇḍit as *Pañcha Tattva* or five great persons.[8]

Kavikarṇapūra writes that Svarūp Dāmodar described Chaitanya as 'Mahā Prabhu' and Advaita, Nityānanda as 'Prabhu'. Svarūp Dāmodar died a few years after the passing away of Chaitanya.

(ii) Advaita

Next to Nityananda, Advaita was the most prominent Gauḍiva follower of Chaitanya. He came to Navadvīpa from Śāntipur. He was the leader of the Vaishṇava community at Navadvīpa. He paid homage to Viśvambhar as the embodiment of divinity. Advaita came to Puri at least three times during the chariot festivals after Chaitanya's return from the South, where he had gone on pilgrimage. On one of the occasions, Advaita publicly declared Chaitanya as the manifestation of all incarnations[9] which annoyed the Master. Advaita long survived Chaitanya.

(iii) Gadadhar (Misra) Pundit

Gadādhar was a close associate of Chaitanya at Navadvīpa. Like Svarūp

[7]C.C.U. p. 191

[8]Kavikarṇapūra *Gauraganoddeśa Dipikā* ślokas 9-12.

[9]*Ch. Bhāgavat* III.10.504.

Dāmodar, he came away to Puri and settled there to serve the Master. He lived at Toṭā Gopināth, adjacent to the Yameśvar temple. He was considered by his disciples as the embodiment of Rādhā. They constructed images of Gaura-Gadāi, Gaur or Gaurāṅga being Kṛishṇa himself.[10] There were such images near the old palace of the Rājā of Puri.

Chaitanya used to attend daily the recitation of the *Bhāgavata* by Gadādhar at Toṭā Gopināth. Gadādhar had some disciples in Orissa. He died shortly after the passing away of Chaitanya.

(iv) Nityananda (Ojha)

Nityānanda left his home at the age of twelve with a monk. He travelled throughout India and visited the Jagannāth temple before he met Chaitanya. Nityānanda accompanied Chaitanya during his first journey to Puri and waited there for two years till Chaitanya returned after his pilgrimage to South India.

After his return to Puri, Chaitanya asked Nityānanda to go back to Bengal to spread the faith of 'love and devotion to Kṛishṇa.' In Bengal, Nityānanda married and settled down to a life of worldly prosperity. Perhaps he thought that asceticism would impede the progress of the faith.[11] Nityānanda and other *Gurus* (preceptors) had a large number of disciples.

Guruship, which became a family affair, radically differed from Chaitanya's ideal of a religious teacher living the arduous life of a recluse. Nityānanda's son Vīrachandra had three wives. He went on horse-back to meet his disciples. But Chaitanya travelled over a large part of India extending from Vṛidāvana to Rāmesvaram on foot.

The Gosvami disciples of Chaitanya at Vrindavana, did not like the changed pattern of Nityānanda's life. In their writings, they were almost silent about him.[12] But after their deaths, there was rapproachement

---

[10]The fantasy has been further extended by describing Gadādhar as 'Gaura prema Lakshmi' (*Gauraganoddesa Dipikā* verse 147). Chaitanya has been called *'Gadādhar prāna nāth! (Ch. Ch.* III.7*)*.

[11]If Jayānanda is to be believed, Chaitanya asked Nityānanda "why do your followers put on anklets and other ornaments while dancing during the religious functions? Who gave you this idea? "Nityānanda smiled and replied '*Kāṭhinya kirṭana* (austerity) is not necessary (for chanting the name of Kṛishṇa) in the Kali yuga" (*Chaitanya Maṅgal*, Uttara khaṇḍa)

[12]Rūpa Gosvami met Nityānanda at Puri (Ch. Ch. III.1.152). But in his poems he never speaks of Nityānanda, though he refers to Advaita in his first *Chaitanyāshṭaka*. Raghunāth Dās Gosvāmī sought the blessing of Nityānanda while on his way to Puri from Bengal (*Ch. Ch.* III.6.132). But he has not referred to Nityānanda in his *Chaitanyāshṭaka* and *Stavakalpataru*. Sanātana in the introductory verses of his *Vaishnava Toshani* makes obeisances to Chaitanya along with Nityānanda *Avadhuta*, Advaita, Śrīvas and Gadādhar, thus suggesting the conception of 'Pañcha Tattva'.

between the two schools of Chaitanyaism, towards the end of the sixteenth century. Though Kṛishṇadās Kavirāj expounded the dogmas of the Gosvamis of Vrindavana in his work, he also highly honoured Nityānanda. Several factors contributed to the rise of Nityānanda to an exalted position next only to that of the Master, though he was Chaitanya's disciple.

1. Nityānanda had a commanding personality. In spite of the temporary set back to his reputation, he retained the leadership of the Gauḍiya Vaishṇavas. Nityānanda was a religious reformer, like his contemporary Martin Luther. Both of them defied the time-honoured custom of celibacy of the monks.
2. Chaitanya was considered Kṛishṇa incarnate by his followers in Gauḍadesa. The conception of Balarāma is a corollary to the conception of Kṛishṇa. Nityānanda, ten years older than Chaitanya, fitted in that role. In the kavya of Kavikarṇapūra written in 1542, Nityānanda has been described as an incarnation of Balarāma (VII.24). Vṛindāvan Dās tries to give a positive proof. He writes that Nityānanda embraced the image of Balarāma in the Jagannāth temple and put the garland on the neck of the deity on his neck.[13] It is difficult to believe that the servitors of the Jagannath temple allowed a companion of Chaitanya to violate the sanctity of the image of Balarāma.
3. His father-in-law's younger brother Gaurīdās Puṇḍit started the worship of the images of Gaura-Nitai, made of Nim wood, in imitation of Jagannāth-Balarāma.[14] Gaurīdās settled at Ambikā-Kālnā near Śānti-pur and made it the most important seat of the Chaitanya-Nityānanda worship. Gaurīdās gradually came to be known as the embodiment of Chaitanya-Nityānanda. In Orissa, he headed the preceptorial list of the devotees who wanted spiritual descent from Chaitanya.
4. From his boyhood, Nityānanda had little contact with society. Consequently, he was free from caste prejudices. 'He had also views which were perhaps far ahead of those of Chaitanya' (S.K.De). He introduced community eating in *Mahotsavas* or grand festivals. Though a Brahman, he took the bold step of initiating Uddhārana Dutta, the leader of the merchant (Bania) community. Uddhārana Dutta was included in the list of twelve Gopālas.[15] While Uddhārana was made a

---

It is stated in the *Prema Vilāsa* (a work of early eighteenth century) that when Gopāla Bhaṭṭa, a Guru of Śrinivās Acharya heard that Śrinivās had married and received an enormous amount as dowry from the Raja of Vishṇupur, he sadly remarked '*khalat pada, khalat pada*':

He has lost his steps! D.C. Sen: *Vaishnava Literature of Medieval Bengal* p. 158.

[13]*Ch. Bhāgavat* III.3.194-6.

[14]Narahari Chakravarti; *Bhakti Ratnākar* canto 7.

[15]Nityānanda before he gave up asceticism, took food even when cooked by

Gopāla, three Brahmans were included only in the list of '*Upa*' (minor) Gopālas. Nityānanda thus introduced a liberal outlook in the Chaitanya sect. In the beginning of the seventeenth century, Narottama Dutta (a kayastha) and Śyāmānanda of the cultivator caste gave initiation even to the Brahmans. Nityānanda's son Vīrachandra opened the doors of the Chaitanya sect to the degraded Buddhist community, then passing through the last stages of decay in Bengal. In Orissa, the Buddhists living near the monastic sites of Ratnagiri and Lalitagiri in the Cuttack district became Muslims to escape Brahmanical persecution.*

Nityānanda gave a higher status to women than Chaitanya who refused to meet even Mādhavi Dasi, an old anchoress, Nityānanda's wife Jāhnavī, daughter Gaṅgā and daughter-in-law Nārāyaṇī had male disciples. Sitā, wife of Advaita, became the head of his Group after his death. She advocated 'Sakhī bhāva'.

Spread of the Nityānanda worship in Orissa

During his life time, Nityānanda did not become a celebrity in Orissa. He came to Puri at least four times and spent altogether about three years in Orissa. He came to Puri about 1520 for the last time. Nityānanda does not figure prominently in the Oriya Vaishṇava literature, except in the *Chaitanya Bhāgavata* of Īśvara Dasa. Nityānanda the incarnation of Saṅkarshaṇa, imparted mantra to Ananta who also is an embodiment of Saṅkarshaṇa (canto 46). Nityānanda's elevation to divinity for association with Chaitanya took time in Orissa. There are some old temples where Chaitanya alone is worshipped.

(v) Śrivas

Śrīvās came to Puri several times from Navadvīpa during the chariot festivals. On one such occasion, a royal officer pushed him for obstructing the king who was watching Chaitanya's dance before the chariot of Jagannath during a *kirtana* procession. Śrīvās, out of anger, slapped the officer. The matter ended there at the intervention of the king.[16]

(vi) Vakresvar Pundit

It is difficult to account for Vakreśvar's exclusion from 'Pañcha Tattva' by Svarūp Dāmodar. Vakreśvar Puṇḍit was a close associate of Chaitanya

---

Uddhārana Dutta (Haridas Das—*Śrī Śrī Vaishnava Jivan* p. 10). Chaitanya accepted hospitality only of high class Brahmans. At Mathurā, Chaitanya ate the food cooked by a 'Sanaudiyā' (a low class) Brahman as a special case. Nityananda is worshipped by the Suvarna Banik community at Balasore in their temple at Kasba.

*Lalitagiri itself is a predominantly Muslim village.

[16]*Ch. Ch.* II.13.177-180

even at Navadvīpa. He could dance during *kirtana* at a stretch for twentyfour hours.[17] The dance of Vakreśvar during a *kirtana* procession attracted the notice of king Pratāpa Rudra.[18]

Kānāi Khuntiā writes that he was asked by Vakreśvar Puṇḍit to compose the *Mahābhāva Prakāśa.* Vakreśvar Puṇḍit died at Puri. His disciple Gopāla Guru founded the Rādhākānta Maṭh. Gopāla Guru writes in his poem, '*Vakreśvarāshtaka*' that his preceptor preached the Chaitanya faith in south India and west India.

III—SOME FOLLOWERS OF CHAITANYA AT PURI

1. Balabhadra Bhaṭṭacharya—He accompanied Chaitanya during his journey to Vṛindāvana.

2. Bhagavān Acharya—He left his family in Bengal and lived at Puri. He often invited Chaitanya for meals in his house.

3. Brahmānanda Bhārati—He was a wandering ascetic. He came to Puri to meet Chaitanya and lived there for some years.

4. Dāmodar Paṇḍit—He accompanied Chaitanya during his first journey to Puri and stayed there for some years. Chaitanya sent him back to look after his mother and wife.

5. Gopināth Acharya—He was the brother-in-law of Sārvabhauma Bhattacharya. He knew Chaitanya while he was at Navadvīpa.

6. Govinda Dās—He was the personal attendant of Chaitanya. He was a Kāyastha by caste.

7. Haridās (Yavana)—He was a Muslim by birth. He became a Vaishṇava for which he suffered cruel persecution. Haridās used to recite the name of Kṛishṇa throughout the day. He met Chaitanya at Navadvīpa and followed him to Puri. He spent his last years at Puri. After his death, Chaitanya himself gave Haridās, a sand burial.

8. Haridās (young)—He was a *kirtana* singer. Bhagavān Acharya his preceptor asked him to fetch some good quality of rice from Mādhavi

---

[17]*Ch. Ch.* I.10.30.

[18]*Chaitanya Chandrodaya Kaumudi*

Prema Das translated the *Chaitanya Chandrodaya* drama in Bengali in 1712 and called it *Kaumudi* (commentary)

Dāsi, as he had invited Chaitanya to dinner. When Chaitanya came to know that Haridas being a monk had met Mādhavi Dāsi, he forbade Haridās's admission in his presence. In spite of the repeated requests of Paramānanda Puri, he remained inexorable. The young monk committed suicide in shame. On hearing this news, Chaitanya commented lightly that Haridās had suffered for talking with a woman. This story, if true, has done great injustice to Haridās and to Mādhavi Dāsi.

9. Jagadānanda—Along with Mukunda Datta, Dāmodar Pundit and Nityānanda he accompanied Chaitanya during his first journey to Puri. He served Chaitanya for some years and then went to Vṛindāvana.

10. Mukunda Datta—Mukunda Datta stayed at Puri, during the Master's pilgrimage to south India. He went back to Bengal along with Nityānanda, after Chaitanya's return to Puri.

11. Paramānanda Puri—He belonged to North Bihar. He was a disciple of Mādhavendra Puri. At the invitation of Chaitanya he settled at Puri. There is a well at Puri which is associated with his name.

12. Prabodhānanda Sarasvatī—He was a South Indian Brahman. He was the preceptor of Gopāla Bhaṭṭa, one of the Gosvāmīs. He stayed at Puri during the last days of Chaitanya and vividly described the love sickness of the Master in his *Chaitanya Chandrāmrita.*

13. Rāghava Paṇḍit—Rāghava Paṇḍit was a Master in culinary art. He used to come to Puri once every year with a basket containing dishes for Chaitanya. This annual custom of sending dishes is observed in the Rādhākānta Maṭh.

14. Raghunāth Bhaṭṭa—He was one of the six Gosvāmīs of Vṛindāvana. He twice came to Puri from Vārānasi, where he lived and stayed at Puri for about two years. Chaitanya advised him to go to Vṛindāvana, where he had already sent Rupa and Sanātana.

15. Raghunāth Dās—Among the Gosvāmīs, he had the longest contact with Chaitanya and was the only non-Brahman among them. He was brought up amid luxury and was married to a girl of uncommon beauty. He left his home in quest of spiritual truth and came to Puri. He left Puri after the death of his preceptor Svarūp Dāmodar and settled at Vṛindāvana, where he died.

16. Rāmabhadra Āchārya—Like his relation Bhagavān Āchārya, he settled at Puri to serve Chaitanya.

17. Sārvabhauma Bhattacharya—He came to Puri long before Chaitanya. His name was Vāsudeva but he was more known by his title of Sārvabhauma which he received for his erudition in Vedanta. His son Chandaneśvar was a follower of Chaitanya. His second son Jaleśvar got the title of 'Vāhinipati Mahāpātra' from Pratāpa Rudra.

18. Śivānanda Sen—He guided the annual pilgrimages of the Gauḍīya pilgrims to Puri. Kavikarṇapūra utilized information gathered from his father Śivānanda, while writing the drama.

CHAPTER XI

The Post-Chaitanya Oriya Vaishnava Literature

THE CHAITANYA faith influenced the growth of the Oriya Vaishṇava literature. There was change in the religious outlook of the poets from the seventeenth century. A new born religious enthusiasm gave impetus to the growth of devotional poetry with the traditional Kṛishṇa *līlā*, especially the highly erotic Vṛindāvana *līlā*, as the theme. There are indeed variations in the details but the poets invariably describe the *saṁbhoga* (love in union) and *vipralambha* (love in separation) of Rādhā and the Gopīs. This standardized pattern gave little scope for the free exercise of poetic imagination.

The Oriya Vaishṇava poets at first gave prominence to the Gopīs. They stressed the superiority of 'Gopi *bhāva*' as expounded by Rāmānanda. But Rādhā eclipsed the Gopīs as the chief object of Kṛishṇa's adoration. The sex passion has been glorified in some pages of the *Rasa Kallola* and the *Gopībhāshā*. Gradually sex lost its importance. In the eighteenth century 'Māthura' poems enriched Oriya literature. The great song-writers Kavisūrya Baladeva Rath and Gopāla Kṛishṇa Patnaik and the great poet Abhimanyu Sāmantasimhāra made significant contributions to the development of the Vaishṇava literature in the nineteenth century.

The Oriya poets did not rigidly follow the general trend of the Kṛishṇaite devotional literature of northern India. Some of the poets deal with the Dvarakā *līlā*, in which Rukmiṇī plays the leading role. The jealousy of the consorts of Kṛishṇa at Kṛishṇa's partiality for the damsels of Vṛindāvana shows the influence of Achyutānanda's *Śūnya Saṁhitā*, X. Uddhava acts as intermediary between Kṛishṇa and the Gopīs who pine for him. Lastly, 'A Kṛishṇaite literature was created by identifying Kṛishṇa with Jagannāth'.[1]

[1] N. Samantaray—*Oḍiyā Vaishṇava Sāhitya* p. 6.

Sixteenth Century

During the reign of Mukundadeva, the last Hindu King or in the next two decades, Dvārakā Dāsa wrote the *Premarasa Chandrikā* and Balarāma Dāsa II wrote the *Kṛishṇa lilā*.

Seventeenth Century

Chānd Kavi or Chānd Dāsa wrote the *Gopīchandan*. He describes the exploits of Kṛishṇa at Vṛindāvana with the Gopīs, which were witnessed by the consorts at Dvārakā. There is no reference to Rādhā except once as one of the Gopīs. The first great Vaishnava poet of the post-Chaitanya period in Orissa was Devadurlabha Dāsa, the author of the *Rahasyā Mañjarī*. 'This is the first work in which Rādhā appears in her full glory.'[2]

But Rukmiṇī is the heroine of the work. *Vrindāvana līlā* is stressed as superior to *Dvārakā līlā*. Kṛishṇa frankly confesses that he loves the Gopīs more than his consorts at Dvārakā. The consorts go to Vṛindāvana and grudgingly honour Rādhā. The first work with a sensual appeal is the *Kapaṭa Keli* by Kapileśvara Dāsa. Kṛishṇa goes to the abode of Rādhā at night, disguised as a woman. After placating her, he spends the night merrily in her company.

Eighteenth Century

Dinakṛishṇa Dāsa wrote the *Raskallola* in the early part of the eighteenth century. 'The direct impact of Gaudīya Vaishṇavism begins from the time of *Rasakallola*'.[3]

The author Dīnakṛishṇa Dāsa describes the erotic episodes of Kṛishṇa with Rādhā and the Gopīs with a background of rich and sensuous imagery. Every line of the kāvya begins with the letter 'ka' which shows great metrical skill. Kṛishṇa goes to Mathurā and stays there. The disconsolate Gopīs muse on their passionate love for Kṛishṇa. They recollect the memory of their love sports with Kṛishṇa in the water of the Yamunā. The intense longing of the Gopīs for Kṛishṇa who had left them and gone to Mathurā has been vividly described. The *Rasakalolla* ranks high in the medieval Vaishṇava literature in India, because of the fluent diction and lyric ornamentation of the poem. In the *Prema*

[2]Surendra Mohanty—*Oriyā Sāhityara Madhya Parva* p. 113.

[3]N. Samantaray—*Oḍiyā Vaishṇava Sāhitya* p. 11.

Pañchāmrita, Bhupati Paṇḍita, explains the theological implications of the erotic exploits of Kṛishṇa with the Gopīs and defends the passion of the Gopīs for Kṛishṇa in restrained language. In the *Pūrnatama Chandrodaya*, Vṛindāvati Dāsi, the poetess, compares moon with Kṛishṇa. whose fullest manifestation took place during his exploits at Vṛindāvana. The simple theme of the poem is presented with a feminine charm.

In the 18th century, *Māthura* poems were written describing the pining of the Gopīs of Mathurā for Kṛishṇa. In the *Gopi Bhāshā* of Danāi Dāsa, the Gopīs express their burning desire for union with Kṛishṇa. The poem is remarkably sensuous in spirit and treatment. Towards the end of the century Bhaktacharana wrote the *Mathurā Maṅgala* which is based on the tenth part of the *Bhāgavata*. It is probably the most popular book in Oriya Vaishṇava literature. The Gopīs lost all hopes of Kṛishṇa's return to Mathurā and spent time in talking about Kṛishṇa. The wailing of the Gopīs at their separation from Kṛishṇa has been described with fascile and elegant grace. Uddhava comes to Mathurā to console the Gopīs and gives a learned discourse on *jñāna* (knowledge). But at the end of the argumentation he admits the superiority of love over knowledge.

In the middle of the eighteenth century, the Marathas occupied Orissa. The Marathas patronized Hindu religion which gave impetus to the growth of devotional literature in Orissa. Sex elements figured less in the writings of the Vaishṇava poets. Sadānanda Kavisūrya Bramā, wrote the *Bhāvalilā Samudra*, taking the theme of the *Vidagdha Mādhava*. In the *Yugala Rasāmṛita Lahari* he describes Kṛishṇa's dalliance with Rādhā and Chandrāvali. The *Chaura Chintāmaṇi* and the *Nishthānilamani* deal with the Vṛindāvana līlā of Kṛishṇa. Lakshmana Misra wrote the *Kṛishṇa Lilāmṛita*. Towards the end of the eighteenth century, poems on *Vihāra* (erotic sports of Kṛishṇa) became popular. Dāsarathi and Kṛipāsindhu wrote '*Vraja Vihāra*' poems. Jagannātha Nārāyaṇ Deo, Rājā of Parlakimedi, wrote the *Vṛindāvana Chandra Vihāra*.[4]

Nineteenth Century

Abhimanyu Sāmantasimhāra was a disciple of Sadānanda Kav sūrya Brahmā. He wrote the *Vidagdha Chintāmaṇi* probably in the first decade of the nineteenth century. The influence of Rūpa Gosvāmī's *Vidagdha Mādhava* is evident on his work. The *Vidagdha Chintāmaṇi* is the last great Vaishṇava *kāvya* in Oriya. The descriptions of Rādhā's musing over her separation from Kṛishṇa, her trysts (*abhisāra*) and dalliance with

[4]S.N. Das—*Oḍiyā Sāhityara Itihāsa*—Vol. III pp. 517-18.

Kṛishṇa show high flights of imagination. The old story is retold with deep spiritual significance. The Rājās of Ghumsur, Dhanañjay Bhañja and Nīlakantha Bhañja, wrote poems on the romance of Rādhā and Kṛishṇa.

The nineteenth century also marks the growth of the *Champu* (devotional song) 'The *Champus* are the best specimens of the Gauḍīya Vaishnava Philosophy'[5] There is harmonious bleṇding of love lyrics with religious fervour. The three great song writers—Banamali Dāsa, Kavisūrya Baladeva Rath and Gopāla Kṛishṇa Patnaik—lived in this century. The intense longing of Rādhā for union with Kṛishṇa is graphically described in their poems. Rādhā represents the eternal woman who yearns for love. In one poem of Banamāli Dāsa, Rādhā feels that she is a different woman after meeting Kṛishṇa. The entire life of Kṛishṇa has been covered by the devotional poems of Gopāla Kṛishṇa Patnaik, which are highly popular. Kavisūrya Baladeva Rath's *Kiśor Chandrānana Champu* is remarkable in its intensity of emotional ardour. In melodious songs, the poet describes the attempts of a female messenger to bring about the union of Rādhā and Kṛishṇa.

The Oriya Vaishṇava literature of the seventeenth and the eighteenth century has been adversely criticized by an Oriya scholar 'as a mass of gross sexual crudities disguised as a religious cult'. Such a sweeping generalization shows that the critic is lacking in the breadth of view. The poets describe the amorous dalliance of Kṛishṇa with Rādhā and the Gopīs with a great warmth of earnest belief. Thei. poems are meant for the devout Vaishṇavas.

To them Rādhā and Kṛishṇa embody transcendental love. They did not consider erotic descriptions to be obscene. Even the morally irreproachable Raghunāth Dās Gosvami, who practised extreme asceticism, gives a luscious description of the beauty and love sports of Rādhā in his *Vilāpa Kusumāñjalī*, without restraint. The concept of morality changes from time to time. The transition from Victorian gown to Bikini has taken less than a century.

CHAPTER XII

The Spread of the Chaitanya Movement in Orissa

THE ORIYA Vaishṇavas generally affiliate themselves with the *parivāras* (family of disciples) of Gopāla Guru, Śyāmānanda, and Nityānanda. A few families trace their preceptorial descent from Gadādhar Paṇḍit.

(i) GOPALA GURU PARIVARA

1. Gopāla Guru—He was a disciple of Vakreśvar Paṇḍit. He founded the Rādhākānta Maṭh.

2. Dhyānachandra—He was a Brahman boy whom Chaitanya liked for his devotion (*Ch. Ch.* III.5). Gopāla Guru adopted him as his successor. Dhyānachandra went to Vṛindavana and probably died there.

3. Balabhadra—The next head of the Rādhākānta Maṭh was Balabhadra. He was widely respected for his saintly character. During his time, the Vaishṇavas at Puri, belonging to the four sects, selected him as the head of the local Vaishṇavas to maintain discipline. As a mark of distinction, they tied cloth of Jagannāth on his head. From that time the *Adhikāri* (head) of the Rādhākānta Maṭh is called Mahant.

4. Govinda Śaraṇa—He was the fifth *Adhikāri* of the Maṭh. During his time, the Chaitanya faith spread to south Orissa. A Rājā of Parlakimedi (probably Jagannāth Nārāyan Deo, who lived in the second half of the eighteenth century) became his disciple. He granted land to build a Chaitanya temple at Parlakimedi.[1] Following his example, some more zamindars of Ganjam took initiation from the

[1]During the passing of the Utkal University Act in the Orissa Legislative Assembly, the late Mahārāja of Parlakimedi, who was then Chief Minister (1936), said 'we are firm believers in the religion that we follow, that is, the great teachings of Chaitanya'.

Mahants of the Rādhākānta Maṭh. There are eight *maṭhs* in the districts of Ganjam and Puri, which are established by the Vaishṇavas of the *Parivāra* of Gopāla Guru.

(ii) Syamananda Parivara

1. Śyāmānanda—He was born at Dharendā (in the Midnapore district, then a part of Orissa) in a cultivator family. The year of his birth, according to his followers is Ś 1456—1534 which is not tenable.[2] His father Kṛishṇa Mandal gave him the name 'Dukhi' (one who is miserable) to ward off evil eyes. From his boyhood Dukhi evinced deep religious tendencies. He heard about the reputation of Hṛidayānanda, who was in charge of the temple of Chaitanya-Nityānanda at Kālnā after the death of his Guru Gaurīdās Paṇḍit. At the age of twenty, he left for Kālnā. Hṛidayānanda was much impressed by the devotion and intelligence of Dukhi. He explained the tenets of the Chaitanya faith to Dukhi, whom he named Kṛishṇadās. By that time Vṛindāvāna had become the chief seat of the Chaitanya faith.

Kṛishṇadās wanted to study the theological treatises written by the Gosvāmīs. With his Guru's permission, he went to Vṛindāvana. He met Raghunāth Dās Gosvāmī, who spent the best part of his life at Puri. He was almost blind at that time. Raghunāth introduced him to Jīva Gosvāmī, the patriarch of the faith. Kṛishṇadās studied the Bhakti Śāstras along with two other young men, Śrīnivās Āchārya and Narottam Datta, under the guidance of Jīva Gosvāmī. The story goes that Kṛishṇadās while sweeping the Rādhā-Śyāmasundar temple, found the left anklet of Rādhā. Next day, Lalitā (one of the female associates of Rādhā) appeared before him in the guise of an old woman. She got back the anklet only after disclosing her identity. The mark of an anklet and a red dot are borne by the Gurus of the Śyāmānanda sect. Jīva Gosvāmī was very glad at the fortune of his disciple and named him Śyāmānanda as he made Rādhā (Śyāmā) happy by finding her anklet[3].

Jīva Gosvāmī wanted to disseminate the teachings of the Gosvāmīs in Bengal by sending their works. The manuscripts were kept in a chest which was carried on a bullock cart which was accompanied by Śrīnivās, Narottam and Śyāmānanda. While the cart was passing through the forest of Vishṇupur (in the Bankura district, in West Bengal) the robbers

---

[2]He was an unmarried young man when he left Vṛindāvana along with Narottam and Śrīnivās. D.C. Sen writes that their departure took place in 1600 (*History of the Vaishṇava Literature of Medieval Bengal*, p. 105).

Hamvīra was the patron of the robbers who stole the manuscripts about 1600 (*C.C.U.* p. 314). Assuming that Śyāmānanda was thirty years old at that time, he was born about 1570.

[3]*Bhakti Ratnakar*, I.376.

forcibly took away the chest, which they thought contained treasure. Śrīnivās proceeded to the court of Vīra Hamvīra, Rājā of Vishṇupur. Śyāmānanda then went to Kheturi in East Bengal along with Narottam. After a short stay at Kheturi, he went to Kālnā to meet his Guru. Hṛidayānanda was glad to meet his disciple and asked him "to make Vaishṇava every family in Utkal".[4] Śyāmānanda returned to Dharendā to see his parents. He married and settled down at Dharendā.

He organized *kirtana* processions at Dharenda. Sher Khān, the *fauzdar* (military officer) at Dharenda, forcibly stopped the *kirtana* procession one day and broke the musical instruments. It is said that he felt burning sensation throughout his body and began to vomit blood. He fell at the feet of Śyāmānanda and became his disciple. Sher Khān was named Chaitanya Dāsa after his conversion.

Śyāmānanda's meeting with Rasika Murāri has been vividly described by the author of the *Rasika Maṅgal*, whose maternal grandfather was a disciple of Rasika Murāri. Rasika was the zamindar of Royni. Śyāmānanda met Rasika at Royni where he imparted initiation to Rasika and his wife. True to the order of his preceptor, Śyāmānanda spread the faith in Orissa. He converted Uddaṇḍa Rāy, Chief of Nrisimhapur and Nabin Kiśor, Chief of Dhalbhum. Śyāmānanda lived for some time at Remuṇā and worshipped Gopīnāth.[5] He also went to Puri and established a maṭh there. It is said that he visited Vṛindāvana again before his death. He had some Brahman disciples like Dāmodar Pati and Murāri Achārya. Murāri wrote the *Vindu Prakāśa* in which he explained the creed of the religious group (*upa-sampradāya*) of Śyāmānanda. The death of Śyāmānanda took place about 1630 at Nrisimhapur (now called Kanpur) in the Mayurbhanj district. The room where he lived before his death, still exists in a dilapidated condition. In the anthology, *Aprakāśita Padaratnāvali*, there is a poem of Śyāmānanda in Brajaboli*, describing Rādhā's tryst (*abhisāra*) in quest of Kṛishṇa. Śyāmānanda also wrote the *Uapāsanā sāra sangraha*, keeping in mind the 'lotus feet' of Jīva Gosvāmī. The followers of Śyāmānanda believe him to be a manifestation of Advaita. In the temples of Śyāmānanda group, Kṛishṇa (called *Madan mohana* or *Rasika Rāya)* Rādhā and Chaitanya are worshipped. There are such temples in the districts of Balasore, Mayurbhanj and Midnapore.

2. Rasika Murāri Patnaik—He was born in 1590 and was the zamindar of Royni on the Suvarnarekha. He was indifferent to the worldly affairs from his boyhood and an early marriage could not change

---

[4] *Rasika Maṅgal*, Pt 1, canto 2.

[5] *Bhakti Ratnākar*, IX.

*Mixture of Hindi, Bengali and Maithili.

his mental attitude. At the age of eighteen he came in contact with Śyāmānanda and became his disciple. Śyāmānanda named him Rasikānanda. Rasika left Royni and settled at Kāśīpur on the Suvarnarekha. Śyāmānanda visited that place and renamed the village Gopīballabhpur, which became the chief seat of the Śyāmānanda sect. For forty years Rasika spread the faith of Chaitanya. He met Baidyanāth Bhañja, Rājā of Mayurbhanj, at Haripur, the old capital of the State. Baidyanāth accepted the Chaitanya faith. He built the temple of Rasikarāya at Haripur. The Mahants of Gopīballabhpur are the Gurus of the Rāj family of Mayurbhanj. The zamindars of Pataspur and Moyna also accepted the Chaitanya faith. A Muslim fauzdar named Ahmad Beg highly respected him.[6] Gokul, a disciple of Rasika, spread the faith in Kendujhuri or Keonjhar.[7]

Another disciple Raghunāth Das preached the doctrine of Chaitanya among the masses in the Balasore district. The *Rasika Maṅgal* (II.7) refers to seven Brahman disciples of Rasika Murāri. Rāmakṛishṇa was the principal Brahman follower. Rasikānanda wrote the *Śyāmānanda Śatakam* in Sanskrit. Towards the end of his life, he settled at Remuna. It is believed by his followers that he disappeared within the image of Gopāla-Gopīnāth.

3. Rādhānanda—He was the eldest son of Rasikānanda. He became the Mahant of the Gopīballabhpur Maṭh. He wrote the *Rādhā-Govinda kāvya* in imitation of the *Gītā-Govinda.*

4. Nayanānanda—He was the eldest son of Rādhānanda. He was directly initiated by Rasikānanda.

5. Baladeva Vidyabhushan—He was born in a Khaṇḍait (Kshatriya) family in the Balasore district towards the end of the seventeenth century. He went to Ganjam to study grammar and philosophy. In the second half of the thirteenth century, Narahari Tīrtha, a direct disciple of Mādhva, had spread his faith in Ganjam. Baladeva was attracted by the Mādhva philosophy. It is said that he went to Uḍipi in Mysore to improve his knowledge. Subsequently, he settled at Puri and stayed at the Tattvavādi (as the Mādhvas were called by the Chaitanyaite Vaishṇavas) *Math.* Baladeva was attracted towards the Chaitanya faith by his contact with Rādhā Dāmodar, an upcountry Brahman from Kanauj. Rādhā Dāmodar lived at Puri and was converted by Nayanānanda, grandson of Rasikānanda.* Baladeva was named Govinda Dāsa. After some time, he was

[6] *Bhakti Ratnākav*, XV.

[7] *Rasika Maṅgal*, II.14.

*In the introduction of Baladeva's *Sāhitya Kaumudi* it has been stated that he was a '*Praśishya*' of Nayanananda.

initiated into monastic life by a monk named Pitambara Dāsa. He now left for Vṛindāvana to study the Vaishṇava treatises under the guidance of Viśvanāth Chakravarti, the author of the *Sārārtha Darśinī* commentary of the *Bhāgavata*. Probably in the third decade of the eighteenth century, a controversy arose at Galtā near Jaipur about the status of the Chaitanya faith. The Vaishṇavas of the Śrī sect at Galtā questioned the orthodoxy of the Chaitanya faith on the ground that it is not affiliated to any of the four recognized sects; and that it has no authoritative commentary on the *Vedānta sutras*. Sawai Jai Singh, Rājā of Jaipur, sent word to Viśvanāth Chakravarti at Vṛindāvana to answer the charges. Viśvanāth deputed Baladeva who was already known for his erudition on Vedanta. He was taught Vedānta by his Guru Rādhā-Damodar who wrote the *Vedānta Śyamantaka*. It is said that he requested the Rājā of Jaipur to give him one month's time. He stayed in the temple of Rādhā Govinda at Jaipur and wrote a commentary on the *Vedanta Sutras* which he named *Govinda Bhāshya*. During the theological disputation at Galtā he silenced the opponents by proving the Mādhva origin of the Chaitanya sect. He explained the metaphysical significance of the dogmas of that sect in his *Govinda Bhāshya*.

In the introductory verses of the *Bhāshya* and subsequently in his *Prameya Ratnāvali*, Baladeva gave a preceptorial list from Madhva to Chaitanya which does not bear scrutiny.[8] Kavikarṇapūra and Kṛishṇadās Kavirāj do not affiliate the Chaitanya sect with the Mādhva sect.[9] Moreover there is definite evidence to show that Chaitanya did not entertain high opinion regarding the doctrine of the Tattvavādis or the Mādhvas. He criticized the Nārāyana worshippers (*Śrī sampradāya)* and the Tattvavādis.[10] Thus it is permissible to suppose that up to 1612, when the *Chaitanya Charitāmṛita* was written, the Chaitanya sect had no relation with the Mādhva sect. S.K. De points out that 'In the Mādhva doctrine, there is hardly any place for Rādhā nor is the Vṛindāvana līlā of Kṛishṇa an exclusive object of attention.'[11]

Why did Baladeva affiliate the Chaitanya sect with the Mādhva sect, though the doctrine of Nimbārka is nearest to the Chaitanya faith?[12] We

---

[8]The names of Īśvara Puri and Mādhavendra Puri, quoted in the *Prameya Ratnāvali* and *Govinda Bhāshya*, linking the Chaitanya faith with Mādhva, are not to be found in the preceptorial lists in the Uḍipi and Vyasaraya Maṭhs of the Mādhva sect.

[9]To Vāsudeva Sārvabhauma, Chaitanya was introduced as a *Sannyāsi* belonging to the Bhārati order (*Ch. Ch.* II.6). Chaitanya called himself a *Māyāvadi* monk on several occasions (*Ch.* II.8.45; II.9.230 : III.7.16). See also *Ch. Chandrodaya*, IV, 40-43.

Kṛishṇadās Kavirāj writes that Chaitanya visited Uḍipi, the seat of the Mādhvas, and humbled them in theological disputation (*Ch. Ch.* II.9).

[10]Chaitanya told Sārvabhauma 'Their doctrines are not without blemish': *Chaitanya Chandrodaya*, Act VIII.

[11]De: op. cit., p. 21.

may suggest several reasons for Baladeva's preference for the Mādhva sect.

(1) The Mādhva proclivity of Baladeva was due to his early association with the Mādhva-Vaishṇavas in Ganjaṃ and Mysore.

(2) There is similarity between the names Mādhva and Mādhava. Mādhavendra Purī has been also called Mādhava Puri (Prologue of Sanātana's *Vaishṇava Toshaṇi*). In the *Vaishṇava Vandanā* ascribed to Jīva Gosvāmī, it is stated that Chaitanya belonged to 'Mādhava' *sampradāya*, which can be read as 'Mādhva' *sampradāya*.

(3) There was common origin of both the sects. Like Chaitanya, Mādhva was at first ordained as a monk of a Śaṅkara order and later on turned a Vaishṇava. He retained his sannyāsa name Ānanda Tīrtha.

Baladeva was honoured by the Vaishṇavas at Vṛindāvana for his success at Galta. He was awarded the title of Vidyābhushaṇ, though he was a monk. The theory of the Mādhva affiliation was accepted by Viśvanāth Chakravarti, the doyen of the Chaitanyaite Vaishṇavas, which gave it a stamp of authority. Repudiation by Viśvanāth Chakravarti or by other Vaishnavas was not possible after the acceptance of the theory by the learned assembly of Vaishṇavas at Galta.

The theory of Mādhva origin was back-dated by interpolating a verse in Kavikarṇapūra's *Gauragaṇoddeśa Dipikā* (21-5) which was written in 1576. But Kavikarṇapūra's drama, written only four years ago, referred to the Master's dislike of the Tattvavādīs. To solve the problem, some lines were interpolated in the drama to show that it was composed in the lifetime of Pratāpa Rudra who died in 1540.

Baladeva was the greatest Sanskrit scholar of Orissa. Apart from celebrated *Govinda Bhāshya* and the *Prameya Ratnāvali*, he wrote the *Siddhānta Ratna* and the *Sāhitya Kaumudi*. He also wrote commentaries on Rupa's *Stavamālā* (in 1764), Jīva's *Tattva Sandarbha* and on Rasikānanda's *Śyāmānanda Śatakam*. Baladeva probably died at Vṛindāvana.

(iii) Nityananda Parivara

In the middle of the eighteenth century the Marathas conquered Orissa. They patronized Jagannāth and Vaishṇavism. Vaishṇava divines (called the Navadvīpa Gosvāmīs) claiming preceptorial descent from Nityānanda, spread the worship of Chaitanya-Nityānanda in Orissa. The images of

[12]The Nimbarka sect recognizes Rādhā as the manifestation of Kṛishṇa's energy (*Śakti*).

Nityānanda were installed by the side of the images of Chaitanya. Gaurāṅga Rāi, a Bengali Fauzdar of Jajpur under the Marathas, oppressed the people. He made provision for his salvation by constructing a temple of Gaurāṅga-Nityānanda at Kapileswar near Jajpur. Affiliation to the Nityānanda-Parivāra became popular in Orissa.[13] Many princely families took initiation from the Navadvīpa Gosvāmīs. Their influence spread as far as Jeypore in the Koraput district.[14] In the nineteenth century, the Rājās of Puri and Bodokhemdi accepted the Gosvāmīs as their preceptors. Families of those Gosvāmīs received lands and settled at Puri and at Dighapahanḍi in the Ganjam district. In the first decade of the twentieth century, Raghunāth Dās Gosvāmī was a distinguished scholar of Puri. Mohan Gosvāmī of the Puri family enriched Oriya music by his devotional songs. In the first half of the twentieth century, a monk Rādhāraman Babaji and his worthy disciple Rāmadās Babaji spread the Nityānanda worship in Orissa. Nityānanda's wives and children, however, are almost unknown to the masses in Orissa.

In '*Nadiā kirtana*', Nityānanda is now invariably associated with Chaitanya. The devotees now sing a kirtana day and night at the Rādhākānta Maṭh at Puri. The first line of the *kirtana* is "*Śrī Krishna Chaitanya jay Prabhu Nityānanda*'. Rādhāraman Babaji has introduced another *kirtana*, the second line of which is: '*Nitāi Gaur Rādhe Śyām*'.

(iv) OTHER RELIGIOUS TEACHERS

1. Sālabeg—According to the *Darḍhyatā Bhakti* by Rāma Dāsa, Sālabeg (Saleh Beg) was the son of a Mughal Fauzdar of Cuttack named Lāl Beg (Pt. II. canto 27) who abducted a Brahman widow and married her. It is said that Sālabeg was at first a soldier. He was seriously wounded in a battle. At his mother's advice he prayed to Jagannāth for recovery and the deity granted his prayer.[15] His poem in adoration of Jagannāth—'Behold the Lord of Nīlāchala'—has been included in the

[13]In the first half of the nineteenth century, Khaḍaṅgā Dīnabandhu Dāsa of the Cuttack district translated the *Bhāgavata* into Oriya. He writes in the prologue of his work that his Guru was the disciple of Vṛindāvana Dāsa who belonged to 'Śrī Nityānanda Parivāra'. Dīna Chaitanya, a Brahman, was a contemporary of Dīnabandhu Dāsa. In his *Sākshi Gopāla Māhātmya*, he writes that he belongs to Nityānanda *Parivāra*.

[14]"The Jeypore family ladies accept initiation from the Vaishnava Gosvamis belonging to the Nityānanda family of Navadvipa. There are numerous Vaishnava disciples (*yajmāns*) of the above said Guru Gosvamis of Navadvipa, who annually pay their visits to receive their *Dakshina* or Mamuls." B. Singhdeo: *Nandapur*, p. 14.

[15]Dr. H.K. Mahatab: 'Bhakta kavi Salabeg: *Jhaṅkāra* (Oriya magazine) January 1978.

Padakalpataru by Vaishṇavacharan Dās, who lived in the first half of the eighteenth century. Sālabeg seems to have lived in the middle of the seventeenth century. His poem on Jagannāth must have taken fifty years to be popular in Bengal. We can guess his floruit by another deduction. In 1692, Ekram Khān, the Subadar under Aurangzeb, desecrated the Jagannāth temple. Ekram Khān would not have tolerated an apostate at Puri.

The *Aprakāśita Padaratnāvali* contains a poem of Sālabeg in Braja Boli. It is interesting to note that unlike Haridās and Chaitanya Dās, Sālabeg retained his Muslim name. B.C. Majumdar in his *Typical Selections from Oriya Literature* has included a poem of Sālabeg in which he says "Let my mind think of the feet of Rādhā-Kṛishṇa, though I am a Yavana by birth (*yātire aṭe Yavana*)". Sālabeg died at Puri.

2. Chaitanya Dāsa—He lived in the 18th Century. He had a Maṭh near the Lokanāth temple at Puri. He was the preceptor of Bhupati Paṇḍita who wrote the *Prema Pañchāmṛita.*

3. Siddha Kṛishṇadās Bābāji—He was the son of Sanātana Kanungo of village Dāmodarpur in the Puri district. His name was Batakṛishṇa. He went to Vṛindāvana in his boyhood towards the end of the eighteenth century. He became a monk and took the name Kṛishṇadās. He served for some time in the temple of Rādhā Govinda at Jaipur. Then he went back to Vṛindāvana and led an austere life. He was the most famous Vaishṇava of his time at Vṛindāvana. To read the works of the Gosvāmīs, he learnt Sanskrit in old age. Kṛishṇadās ordained as a monk a man of princely fortune named Kṛishṇachandra Singh, better known as Lālā Bābu. Kṛishṇachandra came to Vṛindāvana from Orissa in 1816. The Rājā of Bharatpur wanted to grant lands to Kṛishṇadās which he refused to take. Kṛishṇadās is credited with the performances of many miracles. He died in very old age, probably in the middle of the nineteenth century.[16] He wrote the *Prārthnāmṛita Taraṅgiṇī* and *Bhavanāsāra Saṅgraha.* At the request of the Vaishṇavas of Kalna, the seat of Gauridās Paṇḍit, he sent his Oriya disciple Bhagavān Dāsa Bābāji to be the Mahant of a temple at Kalna. Bhagavāna's piety made Kalna one of the chief seats of Vaishnavism in Bengal.

4. Vaishṇavananda Sarasvati—He lived in the early twentieth century. His father migrated to Sambalpur from Keonjhar. To propagate the Chaitanya faith he established the Vishṇupriyā-Gaur Maṭh at Sambalpur. He spread the worship of the Six-handed form of Gaurāṅga

---

[16] Dr. H.K. Mahatab: Siddha Krishnadas (*Jhankāra*) November 1977.

and of the images of Lakshmi-Vishṇupriya-Gaurāṅga in Orissa. He wrote the *Gaura-Govinda Rasāmṛita* in Sanskrit and the *Gaura Lilāmṛita* in Oriya to expound the tenets of the Chaitanya faith. He took initiation from a Navadvīpa Gosvāmī who claimed preceptorial descent from Jahnavī, wife of Nityānanda.

CHAPTER XIII

Chaitanya Worship Today

I—OBJECTS

(i) Foot Prints of Chaitanya

There are impressions on stones which are believed by the devotees to be the foot prints of Chaitanya.

1. Near the Garuda pillar in the Jagannāth temple—Chaitanya used to stand there to witness Jagannāth. The stone containing the foot prints has now been kept in a small chapel within the temple precincts of Jagannāth.
2. At Ādi Varāha temple near Jajpur—Chaitanya visited the temple on his way to Puri. A small temple has been built over the foot prints.
3. At Gargaḍiyāghat, Cuttack—Two foot prints attributed to Chaitanya are kept within a small temple at the Gargaḍiyāghat of the Mahanadi. Chaitanya halted there during his visit to Bengal.
4. At Chasāpaḍāghat, Chaudwar—There are some impressions resembling foot prints on a granite stone on the other side of the Mahanadi. It is said that Chaitanya stood there after crossing the river.

(ii) Body Impression

There are some holes on a flat stone of a big size within the Ālālnāth temple precincts. It is believed that the flat stone contains the body impression of Chaitanya, who lay prostrate before the temple of Ālālnāth whenever he went there.

(iii) Coarse Wrapper (Kantha)

1. At Puri—There is a coarse wrapper of Chaitanya in the

Rādhākānta Maṭh. The devotees took away the shreds of the '*kanthā*' for worship. Only a small piece now remains encased in a glass box.

2. At Santhiā—Another coarse wrapper, kept in the Madanmohan temple near Bhadrak, is said to have been used by Chaitanya.

(iv) Used Articles

In the Rādhākanta Maṭh at Puri, there are a pair of wooden sandals. It is said that Vishṇupriyā sent the sandals for the use of her husband. There is also a '*kamaṇḍalu*' (water pot) in the Maṭh. The devotees believe that the pot was sent by Jagadānanda, associate of Chaitanya, from Vṛindāvana for the use of the Master.

II—PLACES ASSOCIATED WITH HIS MEMORY

1. Amardā—It is said that the Master during his first journey to Puri rested under a tree and took bath in an adjoining tank. There is a bathing ghat known as the Chaitanya ghat.

2. Sundarkuli—Chaitanya spent a night at Sundarkuli near Amardā. He took alms from the villagers.

3. Cuttack—A festival was previously held on Asvina Purṇimā on the Mahanadi bank to mark the presence of Chaitanya. He halted there on his way to Bengal. He ceremonially took bath in the Mahanadi at the Gargaḍiyāghat and participated in *kirtana*. Due to flood on one occasion, the date of the festival was changed to Kartika Purṇimā. It was convenient because the worship of Kartikeśvara falls on that day. As the festival to commemorate Chaitanya's sojourn on the banks of the Mahanadi was previously held on the sands of the river bed, it became known as '*Bāli yātrā*'. There is Chaitanya Maṭh at Muhammadiya Bazar It contains a raised platform under a Vakula tree. It is said that Chaitanya held theological discourse with Rāy Rāmānanda under that tree.

4. Janakdeipur—A mouth of the Bhargavi river near this place is called '*Daṇḍa Bhaṅgā*'. Nityānanda broke the staff of Chaitanya and threw the pieces into the river.

5. Puri—The road from the Rādhākānta Maṭh to the Jagannāth temple is called '*Gaura vāṭa*' (Road of Gaura). The devotees are shown a tree known as 'Vakula vaṭa'. It is said that the tree grew up from a tooth stick of Chaitanya. It is hollow inside to some length. There is a well, known as Paramānanda Puri's well, the water of which was unfit for drinking. When the Master wished the water became pure.

6. Gorapur—Chaitanya halted at Gorāpur, three miles from the Chilka, on his way to the south. The village is named after Gorā or Gauranga.

7. Śambhu Gopāla temple near Dhenkanal—The Master rested there for a day on his way to Vṛindāvana.

III—THE CHAITANYA TEMPLES IN ORISSA

In these temples wooden or metal images of Chaitanya are worshipped. Except one of the images in the Jagannāth temple, all other Gaurāṅga images are of 'Gaura-Nāgara' type, representing Viśvambhara of Navadvīpa. In most of the temples Nityānanda is also worshipped.

(i) Images of Chaitanya Alone

1. Bānki—Cuttack district. It was installed by a Rājā of Banki.
2. Pratāpapur—Mayurbhanj district. According to tradition, Pratāpa Rudra installed that image.
3. Gaurāngapur—Balasore district, This life image of Chaitanya was installed by Baṃśidhar Mahāpātra, a zamindar who became a monk. It is believed that Chaitanya came to this place during his stay at Jajpur. To commemorate his visit, the image was installed and the place was named Gaurāngapur. The image of Chaitanya, made of Nim wood, has never been renovated. It is coloured at an interval of twelve years.
4. Kuans—Balasore district. This temple is situated adjacent to a mosque, which was built by destroying the old temple. The brick built temple of Chaitanya on the Vaitarani will shortly collapse, unless it is repaired.
5. Jagannāth temple—Within the temple precincts, there is a seated image of Chaitanya with shaven head. In Orissa, this is the only image of Chaitanya as a monk.

(ii) Chaitanya Maths and Temples

Ganjam District

1.	Chaitanya	...	Vill. and P.O. Rambhā
2.	Chaitanya Maṭh	...	Vill. and P.O. Buguda
3.	Chaitanya Svāmī	...	Vill. and P.O. Sergoda
4.	Chaitanya	...	Vill. and P.O. Āthgarhpātna near Āskā
5.	Chaitanya-Nityānanda	...	Vill. and P.O. Ganjam
6.	Chaitanya	...	Burligaḍ, P.O. Humma
7.	Chaitanya	...	Belkhanḍi near Berhampur
8.	Chaitanya-Nityānanda	...	Vill. and P.O. Bodokhemdi
9.	Chaitanya-Nityānanda	...	Vill. Nimakhanḍipenth, P.O. Nimakhandi

10. Chaitanya-Nityānanda ... Usthapada, P.O. Polasara
11. Chaitanya ... Bhimapur near Berhampur
12. Chaitanya ... Bhavānipur near Berhampur
13. Chaitanya-Nityānanda ... Vill. and P.O. Digapahaṇḍi
14. Chaitanya-Nityānanda ... Barkatjhari, P.O. Digapahaṇḍi
15. Chaitanya ... Vill. and P.O. Surangi
16. Chaitanya Mahāprabhu ... Vill. and P.O. Palasara
17. Chaitanya-Nityānanda ... Chinguḍipadar near Kodla
18. Chaitanya ... Vill. and P.O. Baragada
19. Chaitanya ... Parlakimedi
20. Chaitanya ... Dhanija, P.O. Aska

Mayurbhanj District

1. Chaitanya-Nityānanda ... Kantakanathi
2. Chaitanya-Nityānanda ... Hatasahi
3. Chaitanya ... Kanpur

Balasore District

1. Chaitanya-Nityānanda ... Mangalpur, P.O. Soro
2. Chaitanya ... Nuāgnā, P.O. Bankipara
3. Chaitanya-Nityānanda ... Dayisingh, P.O. Kaupur
4. Chaitanya-Jin ... Totapadā, P.O. Ghanteswar
5. Chaitanya Mahāprabhu ... Vill. and P.O. Basudevpur
6. Nitāi Gaur ... Bhadrak
7. Chaitanya Mahāprabhu ... Mahapadā
8. Chaitanya-Nityānanda ... Damodarpur, near Balasore

Cuttack District

1. Chaitanya ... Gurudāspur, P.O. Mathasahi
2. Chaitanya Mahāprabhu[1] ... Chaitanya Math, Muhammadiya Bazar Cuttack
3. Gaurāṅga-Nityānanda ... Bangāli Sahi, Cuttack
4. Chaitanya-Nityānanda ... Purushottampur, P.O. Kabirpur
5. Chaitanya Mahāprabhu ... Nilakantha, P.O. Patāmundai
6. Chaitanya Mahāprabhu ... Vill. and P.O. Kapila
7. Chaitanya Mahāprabhu ... Baradā, P.S. Binjharpur
8. Chaitanya Mahāprabhu ... Rampā, P.O. Bari, P.S. Binjharpur

---

[1]According to a record in the Board of Revenue office at Cuttack dated 28 May 1858, Chaitanya Mahāprabhu received an annual donation of Rs. 55 annas 8 from the Maratha Government which was renewed by the E.I. Company.

9. Chaitanya	...	Dubakana, P.O. Mangalpur, P.S. Jajpur
10. Gaurāṅga-Nityānanda	...	Kapileswar, P.O. Jajpur

Puri District

1. Chaitanya Deva	...	Vishṇupur, P.O. Nimapada
2. Chaitanya-Nityānanda	...	Patapur, P.O. Nimapada
3. Chaitanya	...	Chatak hill, Puri
4. Chaitanya Deva	...	Barabati, P.O. Begunia
5. Chaitanya	...	Chhanagiri, P.O. Olsingh
6. Chaitanya Deva	...	Mansibag, P.O. Balanga
7. Chaitanya Deva	...	Banamālipur, P.O. Khandapara
8. Chaitanya Maṭh	...	Taltumb, P.O. Pichukuli
9. Chaitanya Thākura	...	Ghantagharpatna, P.O. Satapātna Via Nayagarh
10. Chaitanya Mahāprabhu	...	Sanagudam, P.O. Kaipadar
11. Chaitanya Deva	...	Robana, P.O. Brahmagiri
12. Chaitanya Mahāprabhu	...	Salatara, P.O. Gediapalli
13. Sonār Gaurāṅga	...	Sea coast, Puri
14. Chaitanya Deva	...	Balakathi
15. Chaitanya Nityānanda	...	Pirjipur, P.O. Brahmagiri

Koraput District

1. 'Urdha vāhu' Chaitanya	...	Jeypore
2. Chaitanya-Nityānanda	...	Jeypore

(iii) Recent Images of Chaitanya

Towards the end of the nineteenth century, the worship of six-handed Gaurāṅga and in the first half of the twentieth century, the worship of Gaurāṅga-Vishṇupriyā became popular.

Six handed Gaurāṅga Images[2]

1. Jagannāth temple precincts, made of Nim wood
2. Old Bhubaneswar

[2]In 1885, the images of six-handed Gaurāṅga, Nityānanda and Advaita were installed within the Jagannāth temple precincts by Pāṭachhatā Ananta Mahāpātra, a temple priest. S. Mukherjee, thirty years ago, built a temple at Bhubaneswar in which he also installed images of Gaurāṅga, Nityānanda and Advaita. The image of Nityānanda is also worshipped in the '*shaḍa-bhuja*' temple at Bārabati near Balasore.

3. Sohela—Police Station Sargarh, Sambalpur district
4. Balisahi—Near Ali, Cuttack district
5. Baladeva temple—Kendrapara, Cuttack district
6. Kesondā Maṭh—Tendakuda, Cuttack district
7. Bārābati—Near Balasore

Vishṇupriyā-Gaurāṅga Images

1. Vishṇupriyā Gaura Maṭh—Sambalpur
2. Gaura Govinda Maṭh—Anandapur, Keonjhar district
3. Gaura Govinda Maṭh—Ghodabara, Cuttack district
4. Jhankarpal—Sambalpur district
5. Ganbharpanka—Sambalpur district

In all these temples, Lakshmī (priyā), the first wife of Viśvambhar, is also worshipped.

(iv) Pancha Tattva Worship

There is an old temple of five Tattvas, Chaitanya, Nityānanda, Advaita, Gadādhar and Śrīvās in the Chaitanya Maṭh at Muhammadiya Bazar, Cuttack. There is another Pānchatattva temple at Bārabati near Balasore.

The Pañcha Tattvas are invoked by the Oriya Vaishṇavas during the *sankirtana* (*kirtana* for long hours) of 'Nāma' (holy names) for eight or twentyfour '*praharas*' (*prahara*—three hours). Five '*kalaśas*' (pots) are placed together and '*tilakas*' (sacred signs)—according to the *Parivāra* of the Vaishṇavas at whose instance the *sankirtana* is held—are put on these pots. Separate *mantras* for *dhyāna* (meditation) and worship are prescribed for each of these Tattvas. 'Nadiā *kirtana*' first began in the courtyard of Śrīvās, in which the five Tattvas participated. This accounts for their invocation during '*Nāma sankirtana*' in Orissa.

The worship of the trinity, Chaitanya, Nityānanda and Advaita is getting popular in the twentieth century. The trinity has been installed in the shrine attached to the tomb of Haridās at Puri by Bhramaravara Jagadeb, a zamindar of Kendrapara. Chaitanya, Nityānanda and Advaita are worshipped in the Āuliyā Maṭh at Puri, and in the temple of the De family at Motiganj, Balasore.

Bibliography

I. SOURCES

1. *Sanskrit*

Kavikarṇapūra—*Chaitanya Charitāmṛita:* Radharaman Press Murshidabad (to be abbreviated as R.P.), 1884
Chaitanya Chandrodaya: R.P., 1887
Gauraganoddeśā Dipikā: R.P., 1912
Murāri Gupta—*Chaitanya Charitāmṛita:* Amrita Bazar Patrika Office 1931, Calcutta
Raghunāth Dās Gosvāmī—*Stavāvali:* R.P., 1922
Rāy Rāmānanda—*Jagannāth Vallabha:* R.P., 1921
Rūpa Gosvāmī—*Stavamālā:* R.P., 1880

2. *Oriya*

(Except the Utkal University publication, entitled *Chaitanya Bhāgavata*, all other books were printed at Cuttack).

Achyutānanda—*Śūnya Saṁhitā:* Arunodaya Press, 1914
Balarāma Dāsa—*Vedāntasāṛā Gupta Gītā:* Utkal Sahitya Press, 1918
Bhagavān Dāsa—*Gaurāṅga Bhāgavata:* Nityananda Pustakalaya, 1967
Divākara Dāsa—*Jagannātha Charitāmṛita:* Union Press, 1916
Īśvara Dāsa—*Chaitanya Bhāgavata:* Bhubaneswar, 1966
Kānāi Khuntia—*Mahābhāva Prakāśa:* Nityananda Pustakalaya, 1968
Rāma Dāsa—*Dāṛdhyatā Bhakti:* Radharaman Pustakalaya, 1913

(The following books are the Prāchi Society publications 1928-33):

Bhaktacharana Dāsa—*Mathurā Maṅgal*
Devadurlabha Dāsa—*Rahasya Mañjari*
Dinakṛishṇa Dāsa—*Rasakallola*
Yaśovanta Dāsa—*Premabhakti Brahma Gitā*

Manuscripts

Mādhava Dāsa—*Chaitanya Vilāsa*
Sudarśana Dāsa—*Yaśovanta Dāsaṅka Churāśi Ajñā*

3. *Bengali (Published in Calcutta)*

Gopījanaballabha Dāsa—*Rasika Maṅgal:* Kavyaprakas Press, 1875
Jayānanda—*Chaitanya Maṅgal:* Bangiya Sahitya Parishad, 1905

Krishṇadās Kavirāj—*Chaitanya Charitāmrita:* Gaudiya Math, 1957
Lochan Dās—*Chaitanya Mañgal:* Amrita Bazar Patrika Office 1947
Narahari Sarkar—*Bhakti Ratnākar:* Gaudiya Math, 1940
Vaishṇava Charan Dās—*Padakalpataru:* Bangiya Sahitya Parishad, 1915-1920
———*Aprakāśita Padaratnāvali:* Bangiya Sahitya Parishad, 1924.
Vrindāvan Dās—*Chaitanya Bhāgavat:* Gaudiya Math, 1928

II. SECONDARY WORKS

1. *Oriya*

Das, Babaji Padmacharan—*Utkale Śrī Krishṇa Chaitanya:* Dutta Press, Cuttack, 1926
Das, Parvati Charan—*Prabhu Śyāmānanda:* Town Press, Balasore, 1936.
Das, S.N.—*Oriya Sāhityara Itihās,* Pts II and III: Grantha Mandir, Cuttack, 1965-1966
Misra, K.C.—*Orissi Vaishṇava Dharma:* Sahitya Akademi, Bhubaneswar, 1961
Mohanty, Devendra—*Pāñcha Sakhā O Oriya Sāhitya:* Friends Publishers, Cuttack, 1973
Mohanty, Surendra—*Oriyā Sāhityara Madhya Parva,* Pt II: Students Store, Cuttack, 1973
Samantaraya, N.—*Oriyā Vaishṇava Sāhitya*—Vani Bhandar, Cuttack, 1959

2. *Bengali*

Das, Haridas—*Gauḍīya Vaishṇava Jīban:* Navadvipa, 1951
Das, Hemanga—*Gambhirā Māhātmya:* Radhakanta Math, Puri, 1965
Majumdar, B.B.—*Chaitanya Chariter Upādān:* Calcutta University, 1959
Mitra, Sarada: *Utkale Śrī Krishña Chaitanya:* Mitra Press Calcutta, 1917
Ray Chaudhury, G.P.—*Bāñglācharita Granthe Chaitanya:* Calcutta University, 1949
Sen, A.—*Itihāsar Sri Chaitanya:* Calcutta, 1965
Sen, Sukumar—*Bañgala Sāhityer Itihās,* Vol. I, Eastern Publishers, Calcutta
Vidyavinod, Sundarananda—*Śrī Kshetra:* Gaudiya Mission, Calcutta, 1961

3. *English*

Acharya, P.—*Studies in Orissan History, Archaeology and Archives:* Students Store, Cuttack, 1969
Banerjee, R.D.—*History of Orissa,* Vol. I: Prabasi Press, Calcutta, 1930
Chakravarti M.M.: Gopinathpur Temple Inscription: *J.A.S.B.* 1900
Das, C.R.—*Medieval Religion and Literature in Orissa:* Santiniketan, Visvabharati, 1952
De, S.K.—*Early History of the Vaishnava Faith and Movement in Bengal:* K.L. Mukhopadhyaya, Calcutta, 1961
Hunter, W.W.—*Orissa,* Vol. I: London, 1872
'Jagannāth Daśaka'—*Bangiya Sahitya Parishad Patrika* (Bengali) 1924, p. 8
Kennedy, R.—*The Chaitanya Movement,* Calcutta, 1925
Mahapatra, K.N.: 'A Note on Yogi Praharaja'—*O.H.R.J.* XII, p. 46, 1953
Majumdar, A.K.—*Chaitanya—His Life and Doctrine:* Bharatiya Vidya Bhavan, Bombay, 1969
Mansinha, M.—*History of Oriya Literature:* Sahitya Akademi, Delhi, 1962

Misra, K.C.—The *Cult of Jagannatha:* K.L. Mukhopadhaya, Calcutta, 1971
Mukherjee, P.—*History of Medieval Vaishnavism in Orissa:* Prabasi Press, Calcutta, 1940
Mukherjee, P.—*History of the Gajapati Kings of Orissa:* General Trading Company, Calcutta, 1953
Panigrahi, K.C.: 'Inscription of Ranaka Ranabhanja' – *O.H.R.J.* Vol. XI
Pillai, S.K.—*Indian Ephemeris:* Madras Government, 1922
Sen, D.C.—*Chaitanya and His Age,* 1922
————*The Vaishnava Literature of Medieval Bengal,* 1917
————*Chaitanya and His Companions,* 1917
(Calcutta University Publications)
Singhdeo, B.—*Nandapur:* Utkal Sahitya Press, Cuttack, 1939
Vasu, N.N.—*Mayurbhanj Archaeological Survey Report:* Mayurbhanj State, 1911

Abbreviations

Ch—Chaitanya
Ch.Ch.—Chaitanya Charitāmṛita
C.C.U.—Chaitanya Chariter Upādān
J.A.S.B.—Journal of the Asiatic Society of Bengal
J.A.H.R.S.—Journal of the Andhra Historical Research Society
O.H.R.J.—Orissa Historical Research Journal
R.P.—Radharaman Press, Murshidabad

Glossary

Avatāra—Incarnation
Bhakti—Devotion
Bhava—Emotional experience
Darśan—Sight of a deity
Dharma—Religion
Dīkshā—Initiation
Goloka—Celestial abode of Krishna
Gotra—Sept
Guru—Preceptor
Kāma—Sensuous passion
Kāvya—Sanskrit poetical work
Kirtan—Group singing of holy names with cymbals and drums
Līlā—Divine sport
Mantra—Words with esoteric significance
Maṭh—Monastery: Religious establishment
Pañcha—Five
Pārivara—Preceptorial group
Prema—Love
Rāsa—Devotional sentiment: Primary emotion
Rāsa—The sport of Krishna with Rādhā and the Gopīs
Sakhā—Associate: Comrade
Sakhī—Female associate
Saṁpradāya—Sect, religious group
Śloka—Verse
Stotra—Hymn
Śūnya—Void
Yātrā—Festival
Yavana—Muslim, foreigner

Glossary of Mythological Persons

Apsarā—Fairy
Bibhishaṇa—Brother of Rāvaṇa, king of Lankā
Chandrāvati—A milkmaid of Vṛindāvana
Durgā—Consort of Śiva
Garuda—Vehicle of Kṛishṇa
Hanumān—Monkey devotee of Rama
Heramba—Ganeśa
Indra—King of gods
Kāliya—A mythical serpent whom Kṛishṇa killed
Kṛishṇa, Gopāla, Gopinātha—Supreme deity of the Chaitanya faith
Lalitā—Female associate of Rādhā
Madanikā—A female associate of Rādhā
Nṛisimha, Narasimha—An incarnation of Vishṇu
Rādhā—Counterpart of Kṛishṇa
Rama—Incarnation of Vishṇu
Rukmiṇi—Kṛishṇa's consort at Dvārakā
Sankarshnaṇa, Balarama, Baladeva—Elder brother of Krishṇa
Satyabhāmā—Consort of Krishṇa at Dvārakā
Sudāma—An associate of Kṛishṇa
Suvāhu—An associate of Kṛishṇa
Suvala—An associate of Kṛishṇa
Uddhava—An associate of Kṛishṇa
Vāsudeva—A name of Kṛishṇa
Viśākhā—A female associate of Rādhā
Vṛindāvati—A milkmaid at Vrindāvana

Index

Abhimanyu Sāmanta Simhāra—Author of Vidagdha *Chintamani* 98, 100

Achyutānanda—One of the five comrades 10, 11, 13, 60, 62-67, 70, 71, 72, 79, 84, 98

Advaita—Follower of Chaitanya 8, 10, 13-15, 17, 20, 24, 35, 66, 91, 94, 104

Ānandin—Commentator of *Chaitanya Chandramrita*

Anogh—Son-in law of Sarvabhauma

Ananta—One of the five comrades 11, 62-64, 68, 85, 94

Baidyanāth Bhañja—Raja of Mayurbhanj 105

Balabhadra—Mohant of the Rādhākanta Math 102

Baladeva Rath—Author of Kisor *Chandrānana Champu* 101

Baladeva Vidyabhushan—Exponent of the faith 60, 70, 86, 105-107

Banamāli Dasa—Oriya song writer 101

Balarāma Dasa—One of the five comrades 11, 15, 17, 62, 65, 69, 71, 75, 78, 79, 89

Bāsudeva Ghosh—Gaudiya song writer 40

Bhagavān Dasa Babaji—Disciple of Siddha Krishṇa Dasa 109

Bhaktacharana Dasa —Author of *Mathura Mangal* 100

Bhavānanda Ray—Father of Rāmānanda

Bhupati Pundita—Author of *Prema Pañchāmrita* 100, 109

Chaitanya, Visvambhar, Gauranga

—Incarnation of Kṛishṇa 1

—His early life 20

—Initiation by Keśava Bharati as a monk 21

—Decision to stay in Orissa 22, 23

—Journey to Puri 24, 25

—First sight of Jagannath 26

—Conversion of Sarvabhauma 27

—Pilgrimage to South India 30-33

—Return from Ramesvaram 34

—Chaitanya at Puri 35

—Journey to Bengal 36

—Journey to Vrindavana 37

—Last years of Chaitanya 37-41

—His passing away 42-47

—Devotion to Jagannath 48-53

—Chaitanya as the embodiment of Buddha-Jagannath 54, 55

—His religious outlook 56-61

—Relation with Pratāpa Rudra 77-79

—Relation with Ramananda 73-74

—Relation with the five comrades 62-68

—Responsibility for the fall of Orissa 79-83

—Influence on socio-religious life of Orissa 83-87

Chaitanya worship today 110-116

Chaitanya Dasa—A converted Vaishṇava 104

Chandaneśvar—Son of Sārvabhauma 97

Dāmodar—Gaudiya follower of Chaitanya 23, 95

Danāi Dasa—Author of *Gopi Bhāshā* 100

Devadurlabha Dasa—Author of *Rahasya Mañjari* 99

Dhyānachandra—Mohant of the Radhakanta Math 102

Dīnakrishṇa Dasa—Author of *Rasa Kallola* 99

Divākara Dasa—Author of *Jagannātha Charitāmrita* 15-17, 69

Gadādhar Puṇḍit—Follower of Chaitanya 17, 35, 91, 92, 102

Gangā—Daughter of Nityānanda 94

Gaurīdas Puṇḍit—Disciple of Nityānanda 17, 60, 63, 93, 103, 109
Gopāla Bhaṭṭa—A Vrindāvan Gosvami 33, 60, 93, 96
Gopāla Guru—Founder of the Rādhākanta Maṭh 75, 95, 102, 103
Gopāla Kṛishṇa Patnaik—Oriya Vaishṇava poet 98
Gopīnāth Acharya—Brother-in-law of Sārvabhauma 95
Gopīnāth Patnaik—Brother of Rāmānanda 82, 83
Govinda—Chaitanya's attendant at Puri 12, 39, 95
Govinda Saraṇa—A Mohant of the Radhākānta Maṭh 102
Govinda Vidyādhar—Minister of Pratāpa Rudra 29, 89

Hamvīra—Raja of Vishṇupur 103, 104
Haridās (Yavana)—A converted Vaishṇava 9, 59, 95, 109
Haridās (Young)—a cenobite 9, 95
Husain Shah—Sultan of Bengal 24, 29, 52, 81, 82
Hṛidayānanda—Disciple of Gaurīdās Puṇḍit 17, 103, 104

Īśān Nāgar—Author of *Advaita Prakāś* 10, 63
Iśvara dasa—Author of *Chaitanya Bhagāvata* 13-15, 17, 64-67, 87, 94
Īśvara Puri—Disciple of Mādhavendra Puri 19, 20, 106

Jagadānanda—Companion of Chaitanya 23, 75, 96, 112
Jagannātha Dasa—One of the Comrades 11, 15, 17, 62-66, 79, 84, 85, 89
Jagannāth Misra—Father of Chaitanya 11
Jāhnavi—Wife of Nityānanda 94, 110
Jayānanda—Author of *Chaitanya Mangal* 1, 5, 9, 10, 22-25, 82, 92
Jīva—A Vrindāvana Gosvami 7, 63, 76, 103, 104

Kabīr—A Sikh Guru 14, 75
Kāluādeva, Kakhāruādeva-Sons of Pratapa Rudra 35
Kālā Pahād—Muslim general 89
Kanhei Khunṭiā—Jagannath temple attendant 12, 28, 29, 75, 76 95
Kapilendra—Gajapati king 23, 88
Kāśi Misra—Temple Superintendent 12, 35, 76, 89
Kavikarṇapura—Author of *Chaitanya Chandrodaya* 1, 2, 4, 5, 8, 16, 20 21, 25, 27, 28, 31, 32, 35, 37, 91, 97, 106
Keśava Bhāratī—Preceptor of Chaitanya 12, 21
Kṛishṇadas Kaviraj—Author of *Chaitanya Charitāmrita* 1, 4-9, 15, 16, 22, 25, 27, 30, 32-35, 49, 53, 57, 75, 82, 93, 106
Kṛishṇadeva Raya—King of Vijayanagar 81, 82

Lakshmī—First wife of Viśvambhar 19
Lochan Das—Author of *Chaitanya Mangal* 5, 10, 12, 13, 43

Mādhava Dasa—Author of *Chaitanya Vilasa* 12, 13, 76
Mādhavendra Puri—Preceptor of Isvar Puri 12, 20, 22, 31, 106, 107
Mādhavi Dasi—An anchoress 9, 75, 76, 94-96
Madhva—Founder of a Vaishṇava sect 60, 105
Madhukara Misra—Ancestor of Chaitanya 23
Māmu Thakur—Priest of the Gopinath temple 43, 76
Mārkaṇḍa Dasa—Author of *Keśava Koili* 84
Mohan Gosvami—Devotional song writer 108
Mukunda—Companion of Chaitanya 23, 96
Mukundadeva—Last Hindu king of Orissa 11, 89
Murāri Gupta—Biographer of Chaitanya 1-4, 6, 16, 20, 21, 25, 32, 33

Nānak—Sikh Guru 14
Nandini—Disciple of Sītā, wife of Advaita
Narahari Sarkar—A Song writer 39, 51, 91
Narahari Chakravarti—Author of *Bhakti Ratnākar* 10, 77, 93
Narottama Dutta—Disciple of Jiva Gosvami 94, 103
Nayanānanda—Grandson of Rasikānanda 105
Nityānanda—3, 4, 7, 9, 12-14, 17, 20, 23, 58-60, 63, 68, 91-94, 96, 102, 107, 108, 110, 112

Paramānanda Puri—Upcountry disciple of Chaitanya 96, 112
Pitāmbar Das—Preceptor of Baladeva Vidyābhushan 106
Prabodhānanda Sarasvati—Author of *Chaitanya Chandrāmrita* 96
Pradumnya Misra—Oriya follower of Chaitanya 76
Pratāpa Rudra—Gajapati king 9, 15, 23, 24, 29, 35, 66, 71, 73, 77-82, 88 89, 94-97, 107
Purushottama—Gajapati king, Father of Pratāpa Rudra 25, 31, 88

Rādhā Dāmodar—Preceptor of Baladeva Vidyabhushan 105, 106
Radhānanda—Author of *Rādhā Govinda* kavya 105
Rādhāraman Babaji—A monk 108
Raghunāth Bhatta—One of the Gosvamis of Vrindāvana 96
Raghunath Das—One of the Gosvamis of Vrindāvana 2, 3, 5, 8, 39, 50, 58, 59, 76, 96, 101, 103
Rāmachandra—Raja of Khurda 89
Rāmadas Babaji—Disciple of Rādhāraman Babaji 108
Rāmānanda Ray—1, 4, 9, 12-15, 31, 33-36, 73-76, 82-84, 86, 89, 91, 98, 112
Rasikānandam, Rasika Murāri—Disciple of Syāmānanda 86, 104, 105
Rūpa—One of the Gosvamis of Vṛindāvana 5, 7, 38, 50, 53, 57-59, 74, 92, 96, 100

Śachī—Mother of Chaitanya 19, 67, 75
Sadānanda Kavisurya Brahmā—Author of *Nisthā Nilamani* 17, 100
Sālabeg—A Muslim convert 17, 108, 109
Sanātana—One of the Gosvamis of Vrindāvana 5, 51, 57-59 92, 96
Sāralā Dasa—Author of *Mahābhārata* 84
Sārvabhauma—A scholar 5, 7, 14, 15, 18, 20, 28, 32, 35, 61, 64, 76, 82, 97
Śankara—Apostle of Śaivism 19, 20, 33
Siddha Krishnadas—Monk 109
Sikhi Mohanty—Scribe of the Jagannath temple 75, 76
Simheśvara—Jagannath temple priest 77
Sītā—Wife of Advaita 17, 94
Śivānanda Sen—Father of Kavikarṇapura 59, 97
Śrīdhar Svami—Commentator of *Bhāgavata* 22
Śrivās—Gaudiya Vaishnava 35, 91, 92, 94, 117
Śrinivās Acharya—Disciple of Gopala Bhaṭṭa 93, 103, 104
Sudarsana Dasa—Author of *Chaurāsi Ājñyā* 17
Svarūp Dāmodar—Chaitanya's companion at Puri 8, 9, 21, 35, 39, 43, 49, 51, 58, 59, 63, 76, 91
Śyāmānanda—Preacher of the Chaitanya faith 17, 84, 86, 94, 103, 104

Tulasi Parichha—Jagannath temple priest 49, 77
Timmarasu—Commander of Krishṇa Deva Raya 30

Uddhāran Dutta—Disciple of Nityananda 93

Vaishnavānanda Sarāsvati—Preacher of Chaitanya faith at Sambalpur 109, 110
Vakreśvar Pundit—Gauḍiya follower of Chaitanya 35, 75, 94, 95, 102
Vāṇinatha—Brother of Rāmānanda 75
Vāsudeva Sārvabhauma—Vedanta scholar 106
Vidyāpati—Maithili poet 31
Vīrabhadra—Son of Pratāpa Rudra 81
Vīrabhadra, Vīrachandra—Son of Nityānanda—4, 13, 92
Vishṇupriyā—Wife of Viśvambhar 2, 3, 6, 19, 112
Viśvanāth Chakravarti—Gauḍiya monk at Vṛindāvana 106, 107
Vṛindāvan Das—Author of *Chaitanya Bhāgavat* 1, 3, 4, 8, 21-24, 27, 29 75-77, 93
Vṛindāvati Dasi—Writer of *Purnatama Chandrodaya* 100

Yaśovanta Dasa—One of the five comrades 11, 17, 69, 85, 89

Index of Literary Sources

Ain-i-Akbari—Abul Fazl 89

Akbar Nama—Abul Fazl 90

Abhibha Gita Govinda—Purushottama Gajapati

Advaita Prakāśa—Īśān Nagar

Aprakāśita Padaratnāvali Ed. by S. Roy 76, 90, 104, 109

Baharistan-i-Gaibi—Mirza Nathan 90

Bhakti Baibhava—Jīvadeva Kavidiṇḍima 78

Bhakti rasāmṛita sindhu—Rūpa Gosvami 5, 57

Bhakti Ratnākara—Narahari Chakravarti 10, 43, 77, 103, 104

Bhāvalilā Samudra—Sadānanda Kavisurya Brahmā 100

Brahma Saṁhitā—Vyāsatirtha 6

Chaitanya Bhāgavat—Vrindāvan Das 21, 22, 29, 38, 40, 48, 50, 57, 91

Chaitanya Bhāgavata—Iśvara Dasa 13-17, 50, 55, 64-68, 75

Chaitanya Chandrāmrita—Prabodhānanda Sarasvati 2, 8, 39

Chaitanya Chandrodaya—Kavikarnapūra 2, 3, 7, 21, 25, 35, 36, 52, 73, 74, 76, 78, 82, 95, 106

Chaitanya Charitāmrita—Murāri Gupta 1, 21, 22, 25, 37, 58

Chaitanya Charitāmrita kavya—Kavikarṇapura 1, 2, 20, 28, 35, 48, 52, 75

Chaitanya Charitāmrita—Kṛishṇadas Kaviraj 1, 4, 5-8, 21, 35-39, 49, 50, 58-61, 74-77

Chaitanya Mangal—Jayānanda 9, 10, 92

Chaitanya Mangal—Lochan Das 9, 10, 82, 92

Chaitanyāshṭaka—Raghunath Dās Gosvami 50, 92

Chaitanyāshṭaka—Rūpa Gosvami 40, 50, 92

Chaitanya Vilāsa—Mādhava Dasa 12, 13

Chātupushpāñjali—Rūpa Gosvami 74

Chaurāsi Ājnyā—Sudarśana Dasa 17, 64, 79

Dāru Brahma Gitā—Jagannātha Dasa 89

Gauragaṇoddeśa Dipikā—Kavikarṇapura 91, 92, 107

Gauragovinda Rasāmrita—Vaishnavānanda Sarasvati 110

Gaurakṛishṇodaya—Govindadeva 18

Gaurānga Bhāgavata—Bhagavan Das 18

Gīta Govinda—Jaydeva 70, 73, 84, 105

Gopi Bhāshā—Danāi Dasa 100

Gopi Chandan—Chand Kavi 99

Govinda Bhāsya—Baladeva Vidyabhushan 106, 107

Govinda Lilāmrita—Kṛishṇadās Kaviraj 5, 9

Jagamohan Ramayana—Balarāma Dasa

Jagannātha Charitāmṛita—Divākara Dasa 15-18, 69

Jagannath Vallabha—Ray Rāmānanda 8, 31, 57, 73, 74, 84

Kaḍchā of Svarup Damodar—8

Kapaṭa Keli—Kapileśvara Dasa 99

Kapaṭa Pāśā—Bhima Dhivara 70

Kāśi Khaṇḍam—Śrinādha Bhaṭṭa 25

Kishor Chandrānan Champu—Kavisurya Baladeva Rath 100

Kṛishṇa Karṇāmṛita—Lilāsuka Vilvamangal 74

Kṛishṇa Kirtan—Chandidas 39
Kṛishṇa Lilā—Balarama Dasa II 99
Kṛishṇa Sandarbha—Jīva Gosvami 7

Lakshmi Purāṇa—Balarāma Dasa 89

Mahabhārata—Sāralā Dasa 13, 84
Mahabhāva Prakāśa—Kanhei (Kanai) Khuntia 12, 28, 29, 75, 76, 95
Makhzan-i-Afghana—Niyamatulla 90
Mathurā Mangala—Bhaktacharana Dasa 100
Mayura Chandrikā—Haridasa 13

Nisṭhā Nilamani—Sadānanda Kavisurya Brahma 100
Nirguna Saṁhitā—Chaitanya Dasa 84

Padakalpataru—Vaishṇav Das 38, 40, 51, 75, 109
Prameya Ratnavali—Baladeva Vidyabhushan 106, 107
Prem Bhakti Brahma Gita—Yaśovanta Dasa 69, 85, 89
Premarasa Chandrikā—Dvārakā Dasa 99
Prema Pañchāmrita—Bhupati Pundit 100
Priti Sandarbha—Jīva Gosvami 7
Prema Taranginī—Sadanānda Kavisurya Brahmā 18
Purnatama Chandrodaya—Vrindāvati Dasi 100

Radha Govinda kavya—Rādhānanda 105
Rahasya Mañjari—Devadurlabha Dasa 99
Rasa Kallola—Dinakṛishṇa Dasa 98, 99
Rasika Mangal—Gopijanaballabh Das 104, 105

Sāhitya Kaumudi—Baladeva Vidyabhushan 105, 107
Sarasvati Vilāsam—Pratāpa Rudra 79
Stavakalpataru—Raghunāth Das Gosvami 3, 5, 39, 76, 92
Stavamāla—Rupa Gosvami 2, 70, 107
Sunya Saṁhitā—Achyutānanda Dasa 11, 12, 61, 70, 71, 85, 89, 98

Thula Sunya Rasa—Ananta Dasa 85

Ujjvala Nīlamani—Rūpa Gosvami 7, 38

Vaishnava Toshani—Sanātana Gosvami 92, 107
Vaishṇav Vandanā—Devaki Nandan 75
Vaishṇav Vandana—Jīva Gosvami 107
Vata Avakāśa—Balarāma Dasa 89
Vedānta Śyamankata—Rādhā Dāmodar 106
Vedānta sāra Gupta Gita—Balarāma Dasa 78, 89
Vidagdha Chintāmani—Abhimanyu Sāmanta simhar 100
Vidagdha Mādhava—Rupa Gosvami 5, 7, 74, 100
Vilapa Kusumānjali—Raghunath Das Gosvami 58, 101
Vindu Prakasa—Murari Acharya 104
Viraṭa Gita—Balarama Dasa 71
Vrindavana Chandra Vihara—Jagannātha Narayana Deo 100

Yugala Rasāmrita Lahari—Sadānanda Kavisurya Brahmā 100
Yasovanta Dāsanka Chaurāsi Ājñyā—Sudarsana Dasa